Praise for *Live Up to Our Privileges*

"Wendy Ulrich's expansive thinking on the subject of women and the priesthood invites each of us to see God's priesthood power in new ways. Her historical discussion of the duties of priesthood will surprise many, helping the reader to think about priesthood callings, assignments, roles, and covenants in new ways. Never dogmatic or prescriptive, her writing has a gentle tone that enlarges possibilities and leads us toward holiness."

—Virginia Pearce, former Counselor in the Young Women General Presidency and author of *A Heart Like His* and *Through His Eyes*

"Wendy Ulrich's book *Live Up to our Privileges: Women, Power, and Priesthood* is thoughtful, sensitive, and well-researched, replete with examples centered on Christ and universal in scope and application. Brimming with an excellent selection of quotations, the reader is consistently reminded of how expansive service in the name of Christ may be."

—Fiona Givens, best-selling coauthor of *The God Who Weeps*, *The Crucible of Doubt*, and *The Christ Who Heals*

"Wendy Ulrich's book illuminates and empowers women to see themselves as a part of the work of the priesthood in ways I have not before heard discussed. Her careful research is impressive, and I love her crystal-clear way of expressing herself. This book has helped me understand that I am serving with priesthood power in ways I have not realized. This is a book I definitely want to share with my daughters and the other important women in my life."

—Bonnie L. Oscarson, former Young Women General President

"Without wresting scripture or tweaking current authorized practices, Dr. Ulrich masterfully demonstrates how ordinary and extraordinary acts that women perform can be infused with holiness and power from God. With a fresh voice, the book explores priesthood functions (typically described and practiced by men) through the perspective of women's privileges and divine gifts. Drawing on her training and experience in psychology, Dr. Ulrich speaks to our feminine fears, desires, and heritage to envision faithful daughters of God exercising priesthood power and authority for the salvation of the human family. A must-read for anyone in the Church who desires to better understand how women experience priesthood power and authority or who feels women are marginalized without priesthood ordination."

—Camille Fronk Olson, Professor Emeritus of Ancient Scripture at Brigham Young University and author of *Women of the Old Testament* and *Women of the New Testament*

"This is a keenly intelligent meditation on and guide to the practical application of its subject. Its reading of scripture and doctrine is insightful without being arcane and accessible without being pedantic. The reader is offered another way of thinking, not what to think about priesthood. Both the general reader and the specialist will benefit from its analysis, as well as its practical ideas for magnifying priesthood in the home, chapel, and temple. I highly recommend it to those seeking a way forward on this pressing issue."

—Kathleen Flake, Richard Lyman Bushman Professor of Mormon Studies, University of Virginia

"Wendy Ulrich is masterful in the way she can take difficult and sensitive topics and excavate them in ways that breathe new life and even healing. As Church leaders have been reframing our understanding of priesthood and its application to women in recent years, in ways that empower women to give their gospel stewardships more forceful expression, Wendy offers a faithful, honest, and personal exploration on how both women and men can better understand the divine power God seeks to endow us with, and how we can work together to employ that power for the blessing of all of His children."

—Ty Mansfield, marriage and family therapist and instructor in the Department of Religious Education, Brigham Young University

Live Up To Our Privileges

Also by Wendy Ulrich

*Let God Love You:
Why We Don't, How We Can*

*Forgiving Ourselves:
Getting Back Up When We Let Ourselves Down*

Habits of Happiness

*The Temple Experience:
Passage to Healing and Holiness*

*Weakness Is Not Sin:
The Liberating Distinction That Awakens Our Strengths*

(With Dave Ulrich) *The Why of Work:
How Great Leaders Build Abundant
Organizations That Win*

LIVE UP TO OUR PRIVILEGES

Women, Power, and Priesthood

WENDY ULRICH

DESERET BOOK

Salt Lake City, Utah

© 2019 Wendy Ulrich

All rights reserved. No part of this book may be reproduced in any form or by any means without permission in writing from the publisher, Deseret Book Company, at permissions@deseretbook.com or PO Box 30178, Salt Lake City, Utah 84130. This work is not an official publication of The Church of Jesus Christ of Latter-day Saints. The views expressed herein are the responsibility of the author and do not necessarily represent the position of the Church or of Deseret Book Company.

Deseret Book is a registered trademark of Deseret Book Company.

Visit us at deseretbook.com

Library of Congress Cataloging-in-Publication Data
(CIP data on file)
ISBN 978-1-62972-581-9

Printed in the United States of America
Lake Book Manufacturing, Inc., Melrose Park, IL

10 9 8 7 6 5 4 3 2 1

*For Barbara Larsen Woolsey and Karin Olson Ulrich,
with deep gratitude.*

*For Maren, Norah, Savanna, Kevin, Aubrianna,
Sonya, Jacob, Anneke, Jonas,
and a little boy on his way,
with boundless hope.*

CONTENTS

Acknowledgments ix
Preface xiii

PART 1
THE PRIESTHOOD AUTHORITY AND POWER OF WOMEN

1. Our Privileges 3
2. Growing in Priesthood Power 14
3. Power from on High 29

PART 2
PRIESTHOOD POWER THROUGH ANCIENT AND MODERN PRIESTHOOD RESPONSIBILITIES

4. Nourish Zion: Deacon 49
5. Build Community and Belonging: Teacher 70
6. Visit Each House with Ordinances: Priest 89
7. Heal and Confirm with the Holy Ghost: Elder 108
8. Govern with Power and Compassion: High Priest, Bishop 129
9. Bless the Rising Generation: Patriarch, Sealer 149
10. Witness: Seventy, Apostle 169

Conclusion: More Than Yesterday, Less Than Tomorrow 183
Index 195

ACKNOWLEDGMENTS

Paul said to the Corinthians, "For God, who commanded the light to shine out of darkness, hath shined in our hearts, to give the light of the knowledge of the glory of God in the face of Jesus Christ. But we have this treasure in earthen vessels, that the excellency of the power may be of God, and not of us" (2 Corinthians 4:6–7). Parker J. Palmer says of these verses, "The earthen vessels are (among other things) the words we choose to convey what we know and believe. For me, the meaning of the verse is simple yet demanding: every vessel we create to hold the treasure is earthen, finite, and flawed, and is never, ever to be confused with the treasure itself."[1]

I too never feel my "earthen" limitations more keenly than when trying to write about the true treasure: the "excellency of the power" of our Heavenly Parents and Savior—power They long to share with Their children. I am deeply grateful to many who have taught me about Their light and the importance of passing it on. I also recognize that this book is only one take on how priesthood, power, and women might intersect, or on what our privileges are

---

1. Parker J. Palmer, *On the Brink of Everything: Grace, Gravity, and Getting Old* (Oakland, California: Berrett-Koehler, 2018), 103.

or might be. I have confidence that rising generations will expand our reach further, and in their own way.

I am grateful to many who have influenced my understanding of our spiritual privileges and the power inherent in them. Monika Ulrich Myers first taught me that you aren't really considered an adult until you are helping to raise the next generation. Carrie Ulrich Skarda reminded me that I am not trying to become a Zion person, but to help create a Zion people. Michael David Ulrich has shown me through his research and example that teams have more power to contribute to the success of almost any endeavor than the most talented individuals. Their spouses, Chris Myers, Michael Skarda, and Melanie Swenson Ulrich, have helped me visualize and cherish what patriarchs and matriarchs really look like in today's world.

As to the principles underpinning priesthood offices, I am grateful to Karin and Richard Ulrich for showing me the deacon-like importance of making sure everyone is fed. To Barbara and Les Woolsey, my most impactful teachers. To Karen Blake, Kathleen Flake, and Chris Packard, who consistently show me how women exemplify the priestly power and compassion of Christ. To the sisterhood in Ann Arbor, Michigan, with whom I first experienced "elder" women's power to heal, pray, and lead (Nancy Brockbank, Lynn Nations Johnson, Marci Nickell, Ginger Bitter, Helen Bauss, Linda Johnson, Sondra Soderborg, Alane Starko, Sylvia Mupepi, Betsy Christensen, Polly Mallory, Kathie Baardson, Lucile Anderson, Janeen Holden, Barb Baughn, Donna Benson, Kris Blanchard, Shirley Thornton, Bonnie Nielson, and Ellen Fisher Nielson, among many others); and to the women of Alpine, Utah, who reinforce those lessons (Dana Israelson, Rena Peterson, Laurel Verhaaren, Cindy Powell, Shauna Anderson, Cathy Lamoureux, Rosemary Lind, Raelene Card, Floy Harley, Georgia Miller, and Teresa Graham, among many others). To Thom Nielson, John

ACKNOWLEDGMENTS

Costello, Wayne Brockbank, Rich Ferre, Richard Heaton, Byron Thomas, Ken Wise, David Klimek, and Allen Bergin for not only showing me what high priesthood leadership looks like but for encouraging me and other women to take it on. To Carla and Sydney Hickman, my sweet Aunt Jan, and my amazing grandmothers, Martha Strong Larsen and Winnifred Cummings Woolsey, who remind me of the reach of sealing and patriarchal power.

I am indebted at Deseret Book to Lisa Roper, a talented, wise, and spiritually sensitive editor, who manages to both convince me she is on my side and spur me to do better; Tracy Keck for her most thoughtful and expert copyediting; Michelle Lippold, enthusiastic product manager; Shauna Gibby for another beautiful cover design; and Rachael Ward for skilled typesetting. I also express thanks to three groups—Laurel Day, Chrislyn Woolston, and the inspiring presenters, staff, and attendees at *Time Out for Women*; my remarkable colleagues at the Association of Mormon Counselors and Psychotherapists; and cofounders Chris Packard and Carrie Skarda along with all the participants at Sixteen Stones Center for Growth, for putting up with my fledgling efforts to grasp and articulate the wondrous truths at the interface of spirituality and psychology.

My deepest debt of gratitude goes to David Ulrich, my best friend, intellectual sparring partner, most enthusiastic supporter, and trusted and cherished partner in the goal of one day receiving all God has.

PREFACE

It is clear to me from both scripture and temple ordinances that God desires and intends to endow us, His children, with His power—priesthood power. What that power consists of, how it is conveyed, what it is to be used for, and how a person grows in it can feel less clear, especially when "a person" is a woman. Recent conference talks have clarified that women are given priesthood authority when they are called and set apart to a position by one holding priesthood keys in The Church of Jesus Christ of Latter-day Saints.[1] I hope to explore what it might mean for women, or men for that matter, to also receive and act with priesthood power.

In the interest of full disclosure, I am a fully committed, believing, participating member of The Church of Jesus Christ of Latter-day Saints. I have also felt frustration at times over gender inequities I've perceived in my Church experience, and I have sometimes prayed with a pained heart about shortages of female voice in the scriptures, Church governance, and representations of Deity. As a psychologist, Church leader and teacher, Brigham Young University professor, mother, and friend, I have also listened

---

1. See, for example, Dallin H. Oaks, "The Keys and Authority of the Priesthood," *Ensign*, May 2014.

to hundreds, maybe thousands of other women and men share their heartaches, hopes, and perspectives on multiple sides of these issues.

Given this background, I approach this topic with some trepidation. I suspect that what I offer about how women can and do participate in priesthood authority and power might feel like "too much"—of little relevance or just more to do—to some women, and "too little"—hollow words instead of genuine power—to others. Both groups may have a point. I am one who *both* finds reasons to believe Church doctrine and practice can support women in reaching their highest spiritual goals and potential without ordaining women to the priesthood *and* deeply wants women to recognize and more fully exercise the power—the righteous influence, personal spiritual competence, and transcendent privileges—God offers us in the Church, the home, the temple, and the world. I hope that looking more closely at the responsibilities and blessings God gives to priesthood bearers may help broaden our perspective on what He wants *from* us all and *for* us all as members of His Church and family.

In Part 1: Priesthood Authority and Power of Women, I'll draw on the teachings of modern apostles and prophets to make the case that women serve in the Church today with both priesthood authority and priesthood power, even though we do not hold priesthood offices or keys. I'll describe some possible components of the process of growing in priesthood power. I'll contrast worldly power and godly power, recall scriptures and ordinances that liken Jesus Christ to women, and examine how women enter the holy order with which the Melchizedek Priesthood is identified.

In Part 2: Priesthood Power through Ancient and Modern Priesthood Responsibilities, I'll ponder each of the offices of the Aaronic and Melchizedek Priesthoods with the question in mind, "Might women—who do not hold these offices—still grow in priesthood power by contemplating and pursuing aspects of the responsibilities and privileges associated with them?" I'll explore ways both Christ anciently and women today help save the human family through the spiritually empowering tasks of

- distributing the food and resources of the Church (a New Testament role associated with deacons; see Acts 6:1–3);
- teaching, visiting, and being with Church members in classes, in homes, and as individuals (the scripturally assigned roles of teachers; see D&C 20:53–55, 59);
- officiating in temple ordinances (done traditionally by priests) and participating in other saving ordinances (done today by priests; see D&C 20:46–47);
- serving missions, conducting meetings, confirming the Church with the Holy Ghost, and participating in the gift of healing (tasks of elders laid out in D&C 53:3; 20:43–45 and James 5:14);
- governing and leading in the work of the Church (a responsibility of high priests and bishops alluded to in D&C 107:10, 17, 68–69);
- helping others discover and fulfill their personal missions and creating and blessing eternal families (roles of patriarchs and sealers suggested in D&C 124:124);
- obtaining personal witnesses of Jesus Christ (a defining role of Seventies and Apostles discussed in D&C 107:23, 25).

By the time we reach the Conclusion, I hope we'll have shared a few glimpses of how women as well as men can fulfill their priesthood-*authorized* callings, assignments, responsibilities, and covenants—*empowered* in the priesthood by the revelatory, sanctifying, life-giving gifts of the Holy Ghost.

I am convinced that God holds out His mighty hands to us, filled with spiritual privileges and blessings. We can hold out our hands to Him, open and prepared to receive.

Part 1

THE PRIESTHOOD AUTHORITY AND POWER OF WOMEN

The teachings of modern apostles and prophets clarify that women serve in the Church today with both priesthood authority and priesthood power. In this section we will consider the contrast between worldly and godly power. We'll consider how women both acquire priesthood authority and grow in priesthood power. We will also explore how women can enter the holy order with which the Melchizedek Priesthood is identified.

Chapter 1
OUR PRIVILEGES

> *Awake, awake; put on thy strength, O Zion; . . . Shake thyself from the dust; arise, and sit down, O Jerusalem: loose thyself from the bands of thy neck, O captive daughter of Zion.*
>
> Isaiah 52:1–2

I remember as a little girl asking my mother for two pieces of bread and a plate. She wondered what I wanted on my sandwich, but I had something else in mind. I sat on the kitchen floor and solemnly broke the bread into little pieces. I was "doing the sacrament." I don't remember if I said a prayer, or passed the plate to my dolls, or just ate all the bread myself. I do remember that during the sacrament at church I could have only one small bite of bread—a bite that always seemed especially delicious—and that I was hoping to replicate that deliciousness and have my fill. I also remember how peaceful and important taking the sacrament felt at church. That was also a taste I was trying to replicate.

I found the look on Mom's face in response to all of this unreadable at the time. As I reflect on that look now I visualize some combination of amusement and maybe mild concern. Perhaps she wondered if she needed to explain something about the sanctity of ordinances and the need for priesthood authority to perform them, which would have probably led to questions on my part, and then perhaps the further explanation that priesthood was for boys. Perhaps I got those messages only later. Or maybe she just brushed this all off as something I would figure out soon enough, just as I brushed it off recently when my three-year-old grandson stuck a doll in his shirt and told me he had a baby in his tummy.

There are both gains and losses to make peace with as we gradually learn what opportunities and constraints our anatomy, upbringing, society, and religion will bring to bear on each of us. Sorting out the fairness of those opportunities and constraints is not a simple matter. Even monkeys get really mad when they are treated unfairly, and humans seem to be wired with similar sensibilities.[1] In a world where the marginalization of women has led to injustices and victimization of many kinds, men being ordained to the priesthood while women are not can seem like an injustice for which God or His Church owes us an explanation. Children have a way of saying it like it is. In the book *Children's Letters to God,* a little girl writes, "Dear God, Are boys better than girls? I know you are one but try to be fair. Sylvia."[2]

I can answer Sylvia with personal conviction that no, boys are not better than girls, and yes, God is deeply and ultimately fair and loves each of us personally and perfectly. I am not just taking someone else's word for these convictions. With Alma, "I have fasted and prayed many days that I might know these things of myself. And now I do know of myself that they are true; for the Lord God hath made them manifest unto me by his Holy Spirit" (Alma 5:46).

I am further grateful for Nephi's clear witness: "The Lord God . . . doeth not anything save it be for the benefit of the world;

---

1. See https://binged.it/2IkRYgX for a hilarious example from a research study.
2. Stuart Hample and Eric Marshall, *Children's Letters to God* (New York: Workman Publishing, 1991).

for he loveth the world, even that he layeth down his own life that he may draw all . . . unto him. . . . all . . . are privileged the one like unto the other. . . . And he inviteth them all to come unto him and partake of his goodness; and he denieth none that come unto him, black and white, bond and free, male and female" (2 Nephi 26:23–24, 28, 33).

However, we're not just being bratty little kids when we whine, "That's not fair!" Joseph Smith teaches in *Lectures on Faith* that if God were not fair and just, it would be impossible for us to have faith in Him. We read: "It is . . . necessary, in order to the exercise of faith in God, unto life and salvation, that men should have the idea of the existence of the attribute justice, in him. For without the idea of the existence of the attribute Justice, in the Deity, men could not have confidence sufficiently to place themselves under his guidance and direction; for they would be filled with fear and doubt, lest the Judge of all the earth would not do right; and thus fear, or doubt, existing in the mind, would preclude the possibility of the exercise of faith in him for life and salvation."[3]

That's a pretty big statement, and it implies that it's okay for us to insist that God be fair. But given the broad range of apparent unfairness and injustice in the world (stemming from our various bodies, families, communities, nations, social strata, financial resources, educational opportunities, etc.), figuring out how God is just and fair must include a broader perspective than this life, and broader criteria than sameness.

The fact that men hold priesthood office in The Church of Jesus Christ of Latter-day Saints and women do not can be either a contributor to or a distraction from our sense of God's ultimate

---

3. N. B. Lundwall, comp., *Discourses on the Holy Ghost, also Lectures on Faith as Delivered at the School of the Prophets at Kirtland, Ohio* (Salt Lake City: Bookcraft, 1959), 121–22. The *Lectures on Faith* were delivered to a school of elders in Kirtland, Ohio, in December 1834. While not written exclusively by Joseph Smith, he reviewed them and prepared them for publication.

justice and fairness. It sort of depends on how you look at it. Some people think the privileges and clout men get because they hold the priesthood favor men at the expense of women. Others might experience the responsibilities and duties of priesthood as a burden from which women are unfairly exempted. While God has not fully explained why men in His Church hold the priesthood and women do not, I trust—and I mean that word literally—that it is not His goal to inflate the roles, influence, or value of His beloved sons above those of His equally beloved daughters. President M. Russell Ballard reinforces, "Men and women . . . are both endowed with the same power, which is priesthood power. . . . Access to the power and the blessings of the priesthood is available to all of God's children."[4]

So I believe Nephi's assertion that, in an ultimate sense, men and women "are privileged the one like unto the other," and that we all have something to gain, not just something to lose, from the way priesthood currently functions in the Church—just as we might have something to gain, as well as something to lose, if it functioned differently.

One thing we may stand to gain from how priesthood functions now is a motivation to look deeper into what priesthood power might mean for both men and women, how it might function for women in the absence of offices and keys held by men, and how what we learn might apply to us all.

POWER IN THE WORLD VS. POWER IN THE PRIESTHOOD

In business settings, power has been defined as the resources available to Person A to influence Person B.[5] Influence is a perfectly

---

4. M. Russell Ballard, "Men and Women in the Work of the Lord," *New Era*, April 2014.
5. See D. B. Bacharach and E. J. Lawler, *Power and Politics in Organizations* (San Francisco: Josey-Bass, 1980).

good thing to strive for. In fact, one way to think about priesthood authority and power is righteous influence in others' lives (see D&C 121:41). But there are also important differences between what power accomplishes in the world and what it accomplishes in the kingdom of God. In the world, having power generally entails amassing money, goods, knowledge, and authority, and using those things to gain influence, approval, status, or control over other people. The ways power is gained and used in this world can make power seem suspect. Many powerful people aren't especially trustworthy with power.

By contrast, in the kingdom of God, the purpose of having power, resources, knowledge, and authority is to pass them on, using them to empower others to get power of their own, become more like God, and enter His presence. This is a startling, game-changing distinction.

The doctrine of the restored gospel about the human potential for attaining godly power is blasphemous to people of most faiths. It is almost unfathomable even to us. But we do believe that we can become like God and receive all that He has and is: infinite in wisdom, goodness, . . . and power. We also believe that one of God's most identifying characteristics is not His ability to create planets, foresee the future, set at defiance the armies of nations, or raise people from the dead, but *His power to share all He knows, is, and can do with others.* He is not limited to creating pets He can train or servants He can command. His glory and power are so vast that He even knows how to create sons and daughters with the capacity to eventually gain the wisdom, virtue, and power to become like Him. These are the powers we trust are possible for us as His children to obtain, including the power to pass on all that we learn and receive about godliness to those we love the most. The purpose of priesthood authority and power, whether embodied in the mighty Son of God Himself or in an ordinary mortal, is to make God's children in every sense joint-heirs with Jesus Christ of all that God has and is.[6]

Yes, we know these can sound like ridiculous ideas, and we know we are utterly incapable of achieving them on our own steam. A lot of us are not even sure we want or would enjoy the responsibility that accompanies such power. But because we love and trust our Heavenly Father, we hope it will work out in a way we'll be happy with. So we try to learn, to repent, and to grow so as to become more like Him—even though that seems more presumptuous than worms trying to learn calculus.

This power to empower, along with the love that motivates it, is a defining characteristic of our Father and Mother in Heaven. This is what God does, who God is, what God desires for us. We accept with awe His promise that nothing can "hinder the Almighty from pouring down knowledge from heaven upon the heads of the Latter-day Saints"—nothing except our refusal to qualify for and receive this gift (D&C 121:33; see also D&C 88:32–33). Power to share all that you have would not necessarily be seen as power in this world, but apparently this holy outcome is the superlative goal of godly power.

POWER IS MORE THAN AUTHORITY

Priesthood power is more than priesthood authority. With *priesthood authority* (authorization through someone holding priesthood keys), women and men can fulfill callings and assignments, represent the Church as missionaries, make covenants, and perform ordinances that are valid. With *both priesthood authority and priesthood power*, they can do these things in ways that magnify those callings, invite the Spirit, bless lives, develop spiritual gifts, and even bring about miracles. Relief Society General President Linda K.

---

6. See Romans 8:16–17 and Doctrine and Covenants 84:38.

Burton affirms, "There is a difference . . . between priesthood authority and priesthood power. Priesthood authority is conferred by ordination, but priesthood power is available to all."[7] (As we will explore later, ordination is one of several ways priesthood authority can be conveyed.) If both women and men can receive, develop, and use priesthood power—and apparently they can—then what exactly is priesthood power, and how do we receive more of it?

PRIESTHOOD POWER IS SPIRITUAL POWER USED FOR PRIESTHOOD PURPOSES

Priesthood *authority* is permission to act in God's name, extended through and to authorized messengers and representatives. It is conferred when priesthood holders with proper keys authorize other men and women to carry out various responsibilities and callings in the temple, in the Church, in the home, and throughout the world so God's saving work can go forward. Priesthood *power* includes all the resources of God's knowledge and omnipotence that can be accessed by men and women of covenant—through the gifts of the Holy Ghost and in the name of Jesus Christ—to use for authorized priesthood purposes. We might need priesthood power to fulfill priesthood purposes such as the following:

- Power to keep covenants we make under priesthood authority (see D&C 45:8–9; 84:42–43; 1 Nephi 14:14).[8]

---

7. Linda K. Burton, "Priesthood Power—Available to All," *Ensign*, June 2014.
8. "We can take heart that our honest effort to keep our covenants allows God to increase our power to do it.

"The fruit of keeping covenants is the companionship of the Holy Ghost and an increase in the power to love. That happens because of the power of the Atonement of Jesus Christ to change our very natures. We are eyewitnesses of that miracle of greater spiritual power coming to those who accept covenants and keep commandments.

"Jesus Christ, our Savior, has suffered and paid for our sins and those of all the people we will ever meet. He has perfect understanding of the feelings, the suffering, the trials, and the needs of every individual. Because of that, a way will be prepared for us to keep our covenants, however difficult that may now appear, if we go forward in faith" (Henry B. Eyring, "Witnesses for God," *Ensign*, November 1996).

- Power to resiliently fulfill our foreordained mission and our priesthood-assigned work on earth (see D&C 138:55–56; Moses 1:6; Alma 26:15).
- Power to receive a fullness of the Holy Ghost (see D&C 109:15; 121:46).
- Power to build and strengthen covenant relationships within families, wards, Relief Societies, priesthood quorums, Young Women classes, presidencies, and councils.[9]
- Power to bless any and all of God's children in our families, wards and branches, communities, nations, and throughout the world.[10]
- Power to know God, speak and act in His name, come into His presence, and be resurrected with His glory (see John 14:13–14; D&C 84:19–24; Moses 7:13, 59–60).
- Power to influence and empower others for good eternally, especially those we love (see Moses 1:38–39; D&C 121:41, 46; 132:19–20).

This list and related scriptures and quotations are packed with crucial contexts and motivations for learning and exercising true spiritual power.

LIVING BENEATH, LIVING UP

Brigham Young notes that the Saints in his day were living far beneath the privileges listed above: "There is no doubt, if a person lives according to the revelations given to God's people, he may have the Spirit of the Lord to signify to him his will, and to guide and to direct him in the discharge of his duties, in his temporal as

---

9. See Dallin H. Oaks, "Priesthood Authority in the Family and the Church," *Ensign*, October 2005.
10. "Love . . . ought to be manifested by those who aspire to be the sons of God. A man filled with the love of God, is not content with blessing his family alone, but ranges through the whole world, anxious to bless the whole human race" (Joseph Smith, in Larry E. Dahl and Donald Q. Cannon, eds., *Encyclopedia of Joseph Smith's Teachings* [Salt Lake City: Deseret Book, 2000], 107).

well as his spiritual exercises. I am satisfied, however, that in this respect, *we live far beneath our privileges.*"[11]

More recently, Elder Dieter F. Uchtdorf has elaborated on this theme to priesthood bearers specifically: "The more we study the purpose, potential, and practical use of the priesthood, the more we will be amazed by its power, and the Spirit will teach us how to access and use that power to bless our families, our communities, and the Church. . . . We *live beneath our privileges* when we fail to partake of the feast of happiness, peace, and joy that God grants so bountifully to faithful priesthood servants."[12]

Similar comments were made to priesthood bearers by President Boyd K. Packer: "Too many of our priesthood brethren are *living below their privileges* and the Lord's expectations.

"We must go forward, confident of the supernal power of the priesthood. It is a source of strength and encouragement to know who we are and what we have and what we must do in the work of the Almighty."[13]

President Russell M. Nelson has also said: "Too many of our brothers and sisters do not fully understand the concept of priesthood power and authority. They act as though they would rather satisfy their own selfish desires and appetites than use the power of God to bless His children.

"I fear that too many of our brothers and sisters *do not grasp the privileges* that could be theirs."[14]

But the very first reference to living up to our privileges, as near as I can tell, is in Joseph Smith's prophetic words to the women of the newly organized Relief Society: "It is natural for

---

11. Brigham Young, in *Discourses of Brigham Young,* sel. and arr. by John A. Widtsoe (Salt Lake City: Deseret Book, 1973), 32; emphasis added.
12. Dieter F. Uchtdorf, "Your Potential, Your Privilege," *Ensign,* April 2011; emphasis added.
13. Boyd K. Packer, "The Power of the Priesthood," *Ensign,* May 2010; emphasis added.
14. Russell M. Nelson, "Ministering with the Power and Authority of God," *Ensign,* May 2018; emphasis added.

females to have feelings of charity—you are now placed in a situation where you can act according to those sympathies which God has planted in your bosoms. If you live up to these principles how great and glorious!—*if you live up to your privileges*, angels cannot be restrained from being your associates—females, if they are pure and innocent can come into the presence of God."[15]

These promises to the women of the Church mirror the promises associated with the Aaronic and Melchizedek Priesthoods: the ministering of angels; the presence of God (see D&C 84:19–23, 26). These startling privileges completely reframe the purposes of our participation in the Relief Society, as well as the meaning and potential of our entire earthly experience. We live up to these privileges when we recognize the priesthood authority we can be given as women or men, participate in God's work of saving and exalting His children, establish eternal families, complete our individual missions on earth, build Zion, raise the next generations of faithful Saints, and prepare the earth for the millennial reign of the Lord Jesus Christ. We live up to these privileges when we exercise our agency to grow spiritually and qualify for the gifts of the Holy Ghost so that we can act and speak with power. We live up to our privileges when we take the journey of faith and courage that culminates in coming into the presence of God and Christ and receiving all that They have.

God's promised blessings are reaffirmed by President M. Russell Ballard: "All who have made sacred covenants with the Lord and who honor those covenants are eligible to receive personal revelation, to be blessed by the ministering of angels, to commune with God, to receive the fulness of the gospel, and, ultimately, to become heirs alongside Jesus Christ of all our Father has."[16]

---

15. Joseph Smith, in Relief Society Minute Book, Nauvoo, Illinois, April 28, 1842, 38–39; emphasis added.
16. M. Russell Ballard, "Men and Women and Priesthood Power," *Ensign*, September 2014.

These promises are ours.

When as a little girl I broke bread onto a plate trying to replicate the sacrament, I had no concept of the privileges that awaited me as a daughter of God. While I do not act in the specific priestly role I imitated then, the priesthood-authorized callings and assignments I have filled and the priesthood promises I confidently seek infinitely surpass anything I then imagined. I once hoped to replicate the delicious taste of that little morsel of bread I was offered during the sacrament. God offers me the whole delicious loaf, the recipe, the ingredients, the bakery, and all the deep, unfathomable spiritual realities they represent. I can develop my own relationship with heaven, and help those I love most to do the same, forever. I want to say to that little girl from all those years ago, "Just wait. There is so much for you to do and have and be as you 'grow up in God'[17] in this Church. Just wait!"

---

17. See Doctrine and Covenants 109:15.

Chapter 2

GROWING IN PRIESTHOOD POWER

And it came to pass that I, Nephi, beheld the power of the Lamb of God, that it descended . . . upon the covenant people of the Lord . . . ; and they were armed with righteousness and with the power of God in great glory.

1 Nephi 14:14

Priesthood power is the power to do God's work in the world. The purpose of this power is not just to bless the Church but to bless all of God's children. As people of covenant, we are entitled to that power in every good work we undertake for the benefit of the human family. Priesthood power comes into our lives when we align our skills and our wills with those of Jesus Christ, the Holy Ghost, and God for the holy purpose of saving and lifting humankind. To develop priesthood power thus requires both 1) pondering what matters most, taking creative risks, exercising agency, working hard, and resiliently trying again in the face of setbacks as we grow in spiritual skills; and 2) access to the will and skill of God, harnessed and lent to us on His terms and for His purposes.

How does priesthood power differ from or relate to the power of faith, the power of the Holy Ghost, the power of the Atonement of Christ, the power of charity, the power of prayer, or the power of personal preparation and righteousness? I'm not completely sure. Maybe that is a little like asking how the power of a jet plane differs from or relates to the power of the jet engines, the power of the fuel, the power of the shape and contour of the wings that create lift, the power of the computer systems and controls, the power of the engineer who designed the plane, or the power of the trained pilot who guides it. All these aspects of the jet plane's flight (and more) contribute to its power. And by "contribute to" I don't just mean "add to." If any of these essential parts were missing, the entire plane would become utterly powerless.

At least four individuals—a mortal child of God, the Savior Jesus Christ, the Holy Ghost, and God the Father—work together to bring priesthood power and blessings into our lives and to empower us to empower others. These seem to be the roles of each individual in that process:

1. We, as the mortal child of God, choose to grow in character and holiness. This includes exercising faith in Christ and His Atonement; repenting; and receiving baptism, the gift of the Holy Ghost, and temple ordinances. It includes serving with love, purifying our intentions, and growing in spiritual skills as we struggle with the weaknesses inherent in our mortal state.

2. Jesus Christ gives us priesthood authority through those holding priesthood keys, allowing us (as called to do so) to act in His name, teach His doctrine, help govern His Church, and perform the ordinances of salvation and exaltation that help create holy individuals, Zion communities, and eternal families.

3. The Holy Ghost gives us gifts to tutor us in spiritual power. The Holy Ghost is a testator, comforter, and sanctifier. His gifts include revelation, prophecy, healing, teaching, administration, visions, and all kinds of miracles. The gift and gifts of the Holy Ghost help us receive personal revelation to magnify our priesthood-authorized work with spiritual power.

4. By covenant, God promises us astounding blessings. When we receive God's authority and power, receive God's messengers, and receive God's Son, God promises us the ministering of angels and His own presence, both here and in eternity. We in turn become ministers and messengers to others, empowering them to join us on the path to exaltation.

Let's explore these points in more detail.

WE CHOOSE TO GROW IN CHARACTER AND HOLINESS

Our journey to power in the priesthood begins with faith in Christ, repentance, baptism, and the gift of the Holy Ghost. It proceeds as we continue to use our agency to become more spiritually skilled and pure-hearted as disciples of Jesus Christ.

Sincerely repenting of our sins of rebellion or disobedience allows us to be forgiven and to be clean again through the Atonement of Jesus Christ (see Moroni 6:8). But sin is not our only challenge in mortality. We also struggle with the weakness of simply being human. It feels crucial to remember that, ironically, it is through our mortal experience with weakness, blessed by the redemptive grace of Jesus Christ, that we are eventually made strong—that is, given godly power as men and women of covenant until eventually we are prepared to "inherit thrones, kingdoms, principalities, and powers, dominions, all heights and depths . . . ; and they shall pass by the angels, and the gods, which are set there, to their exaltation and glory in all things, as hath been sealed upon their heads, which glory shall be a fulness and a continuation of the seeds forever and ever. Then shall they be gods, because they have no end; therefore shall they be from everlasting to everlasting, because they continue; then shall they be above all, because all things are subject unto them. Then shall they be gods, because they have all power" (D&C 132:19–20).

Apparently our long experience with God in the premortal

world was not enough to qualify us for such power; our mortal experiences with weakness and powerlessness are essential. We come into this world as tiny babies whose very lives depend on others. We must borrow the skills and resources of others over the course of many years before we can even survive on our own. We carry the lessons of that powerlessness, and sometimes its scars, all our lives. Young, powerless children may especially benefit from having mothers and fathers who have personal experience with, and compassion for, powerlessness. The Church and society at large also benefit when people familiar with the frustrations, losses, threats, and despairs of powerlessness bring their perspectives and compassion to the tables of power.

Weakness includes limitations and infirmities, such as physical and emotional illness and predispositions, lack of skill or wisdom, inadequate stamina or resilience, self-limiting conclusions we draw from bad experiences or faulty teaching, and susceptibility to temptation. Our humility and faith in Christ qualify us for His grace, the enabling power by which He can "make weak things become strong" in us (Ether 12:27).

A story from the life of President Russell M. Nelson demonstrates powerfully the gradual process of growth in skill and power. While the power he sought at this time was healing power, the process he engaged in applies to learning any spiritual power. That process includes experience, practice, careful thought, the help of others, stamina, prayer, and compassion for others and for ourselves as we learn from difficult failures.

In the early days of innovating open-heart surgery, President Nelson, then a full-time doctor, was asked to operate on the heart of a child who was very ill with congenital heart disease. One child in this family had already died from this disease before these surgery techniques had become available. A second child with the disease had died when Doctor Nelson had attempted surgery. Now the family brought this third child to him. I cannot even imagine how fervently he must have prayed and studied and hoped for the gift and power of healing for this little girl and her family. He performed the operation, apparently with good success, but a few hours later this third child also died.

President Nelson writes: "I went home grief stricken. I threw myself upon our living room floor and cried all night long. Dantzel [my wife] stayed by my side, listening as I repeatedly declared that I would never perform another heart operation. Then, around 5:00 in the morning, Dantzel looked at me and lovingly asked, 'Are you finished crying? Then get dressed. Go back to the lab. Go to work! You need to learn more. If you quit now, others will have to painfully learn what you already know.'"[1]

This is not just a good story about the power or influence of a righteous woman, although it is that. It is also a good story about the way we feel when we are exercising our agency to do new things—hard things—and when we fail. It is a story about how we grow in spiritual power by trying to solve problems we don't know how to solve, understand doctrine we don't yet understand, take on roles we are not sure how to assume, and try to bring spiritual gifts to life that take practice and even risk to develop (such as learning to serve with generosity without enabling dependence, or learning to attend to spiritual promptings without seeing every thought that crosses our mind as coming straight from God). We, with pioneers of all kinds, must be willing to rewrite the old adage, "If a thing is worth doing, it is worth doing well." Perhaps more accurately, if a thing is worth doing, it is worth doing *badly* while we learn to do it better, rather than not doing it at all. But we will have to learn to get up and try again, no matter how serious our errors, if we are to get better at important, even spiritually crucial, things we currently

---

1. Russell M. Nelson, "A Plea to My Sisters," *Ensign*, November 2015.

do not know how to do—things like parenting, forgiving, sharing the gospel, praying, ministering, magnifying Church callings, being a student of the scriptures, building community, or being confident but humble, to name a few. Exercising spiritual power is one such thing. We can rely on the Lord's promise that the "doctrine of the priesthood shall distil upon thy soul as the dews from heaven" as we practice the principles on which that distilling depends (D&C 121:45; see also verses 34–46). But distilling is a slow and delicate process.

Once, when Christ's Apostles came across someone they couldn't heal, Christ had to step in to do the job. When they asked Him why they had failed even though they had proper authority, He told them, "Because of your unbelief," adding, "this kind goeth not out but by prayer and fasting" (Matthew 17:20–21). Fasting and prayer didn't give the Apostles any more authority, but we can imagine that fasting and prayer might have increased their power, tutoring them in faith, humility, discipline, and pure intentions and stripping off the distractions of this world.

Joseph Smith taught that sacrifice is also essential to building faith and spiritual power.[2] Ed J. Pinegar states, "True worship always includes both calling on the name of the Lord and sacrifice on our part."[3] I find it worth prayerfully pondering what the sacrifice is the Lord is asking of me at any given time so that I can better serve and grow. President Nelson and his family sacrificed greatly so he could develop the skills and power to save lives, physically and spiritually. Anyone who wants the skills to make a difference for good and to live a meaningful life must sacrifice.

---

2. See *Lectures on Faith*, 6:7, in *Encyclopedia of Joseph Smith's Teachings*, ed. L. E. Dahl and D. Q. Cannon (Salt Lake City: Bookcraft, 1997), 590–91.
3. Ed J. Pinegar, *The Temple: Gaining Knowledge and Power in the House of the Lord* (American Fork, Utah: Covenant Communications, 2014), 98.

JESUS CHRIST GIVES US PRIESTHOOD AUTHORITY THROUGH THOSE HOLDING PRIESTHOOD KEYS

As our spiritual growth unfolds, we are given more opportunities to grow and learn, including through assignments and callings that come through those holding priesthood keys. When we think of priesthood as something that is only the prerogative of men, women can seem to be excluded from power and authority to act in the name of God. Learning that women also have this power and authority, we may wonder exactly what men have that women do not. President Dallin H. Oaks includes in his description of priesthood, "the power by which we will be resurrected and proceed to eternal life," "the power by which the earth was created," and the "consummate power on earth."[4] The power to resurrect the dead, create planets, or govern the entire world is certainly impressive, but *way* above my pay grade. And yours, whether you're a man or a woman. Fortunately, President Oaks also quotes President Joseph F. Smith's description of priesthood as "the power of God delegated to man by which man can act in the earth for the salvation of the human family."[5] That's a little closer to something I, a mere mortal, might dare to aspire to participate in. I can surely take some action toward the salvation of the human family! (I also note that in this definition this godly power is delegated to "man," not to "men." In his day, that implied *humans*, not just males.)

We learn: "The Melchizedek Priesthood holds the right of presidency, and has power and authority over all the offices in the church in all ages of the world, to administer in spiritual things. . . . The power and authority of the . . . Melchizedek Priesthood [includes] the privilege of receiving the mysteries of the kingdom of heaven, to have the heavens opened unto them, to commune with

---

4. Dallin H. Oaks, "The Keys and Authority of the Priesthood," *Ensign*, May 2014.
5. Joseph Fielding Smith, ed., *Gospel Doctrine: Selections from the Sermons and Writings of Joseph F. Smith*, 5th ed. (Salt Lake City: Deseret Book, 1939), 139.

the general assembly and church of the Firstborn, and to enjoy the communion and presence of God the Father, and Jesus the mediator of the new covenant. The power and authority of the . . . Aaronic Priesthood, is to hold the keys of the ministering of angels, and to administer in outward ordinances" (D&C 107:8, 18–20).

These are heady promises that I think a person would be crazy *not* to desire. And this is where things start to get tricky. If priesthood is held by men and not women, which in some ways it clearly is, then are women relegated to the cheering section to root for the right team, or do we actually get to put on jerseys and play?

I have struggled to find a definition of priesthood that clarifies what men have that women do not. Is priesthood what authorizes performing ordinances? Yes, but women are authorized to perform and officiate in the highest order of priesthood ordinances: temple ordinances. Maybe priesthood is necessary to lead. Yes, but women clearly lead with authority and power in Relief Society, in Young Women, and in the home. Well then, maybe priesthood is necessary to govern mixed-sex groups. But women not only direct the mixed-sex children in the Primary organization, but they direct the mixed-sex adults who teach those children. Does priesthood have to do with the duties associated with priesthood offices, then? Yes, but covenant women operate in various ways in virtually all of the capacities that the names and descriptions of priesthood offices imply, as will be discussed in Part 2.

I have finally given up trying to define priesthood in a way that unilaterally distinguishes what men have that women do not, although there is pretty clearly *something* crucial given to men as part of these priesthood offices and keys that is different from what is given to women. For example, priesthood offices held by men come with certain responsibilities and duties that women are not obligated to assume. These offices are cumulative, and one is not released from a priesthood office as one is from a calling. Also, some men holding the priesthood are given keys to oversee a ward, stake, temple, mission, or area, and women are not given keys. But frankly, neither do most male priesthood holders hold keys at any given point in time.

In any case, President M. Russell Ballard clarifies: "Those who have priesthood keys . . . literally make it possible for all who serve faithfully under their direction to exercise priesthood authority and have access to priesthood power."[6]

President Dallin H. Oaks further elaborates: "Every act or ordinance performed in the Church is done under the direct or indirect authorization of one holding the keys for that function. . . .

"In the controlling of the exercise of priesthood authority, the function of priesthood keys both enlarges and limits. It enlarges by making it possible for priesthood authority and blessings to be available for all of God's children. It limits by directing who will be given the authority of the priesthood, who will hold its offices, and how its rights and powers will be conferred. For example, a person who holds the priesthood is not able to confer his office or authority on another unless authorized by one who holds the keys. Without that authorization, the ordination would be invalid. This explains why a priesthood holder—regardless of office—cannot ordain a member of his family or administer the sacrament in his own home without authorization from the one who holds the appropriate keys."[7]

So while only certain men hold keys, the purpose of those keys is to ensure that both men and women can operate with priesthood authority and power in the work of the Lord. In the end, then, I wonder if it would be more helpful for most purposes to simply define priesthood as the power and authority given in different ways to men and women in God's Church to administer the affairs

---

6. In Oaks, "The Keys and Authority of the Priesthood."
7. Oaks, "The Keys and Authority of the Priesthood."

of His kingdom, teach His doctrine, and perform priesthood ordinances of salvation and exaltation as they "act in the earth for the salvation of the human family" under the direction of those holding priesthood keys.

Priesthood authority and priesthood power are different, though, and a person can have one without the other. I think of conversations I've had with women over the years in which one of us has complained, "I work pretty hard to have the Spirit, to understand the doctrine, and to magnify the callings I'm given. It doesn't feel like this man I have to work with (or under) is pulling his weight. Why does he have the decision-making authority when he doesn't work as hard as I do to have the Spirit?" Indeed, I have listened to or read priesthood sessions of general conference enough to note that men also remind each other that they can't afford to rest on the laurels of having priesthood authority; they need to also work to attain the spiritual power to go with it. Authority without spiritual power is a problem.

From President Boyd K. Packer: "We have done very well at distributing the *authority* of the priesthood. We have priesthood authority planted nearly everywhere. We have quorums of elders and high priests worldwide. But distributing the *authority* of the priesthood has raced, I think, ahead of distributing the *power* of the priesthood. The priesthood does not have the strength that it should have and will not have until the *power* of the priesthood is firmly fixed in the families as it should be."[8]

Women, in contrast, are often publicly lauded for excelling in righteousness and spiritual gifts, implying to some that they have innate spiritual power so they don't need priesthood authority.

---

8. "The Power of the Priesthood," *Ensign*, May 2010. I'm curious as to what President Packer means by fixing the power of the priesthood "in the families" as opposed to in the quorums or individual men. Unfortunately, he is no longer here to ask, but it sounds like he envisioned priesthood power as belonging and developing in a particular way in the family with all its constituents.

That can feel to some like a placating attempt to justify excluding women from the tables of decision-making and influence. Spiritual power without authority would also be a problem.

More recent statements by apostles and prophets seem to clarify that women and men can *both* have *both* authority and power in the priesthood, and that we all need both in order to fulfill our responsibilities and privileges in the kingdom of God.

President Dallin H. Oaks clarifies: "We are not accustomed to speaking of women having the authority of the priesthood in their Church callings, but what other authority can it be? When a woman—young or old—is set apart to preach the gospel as a full-time missionary, she is given priesthood authority to perform a priesthood function. The same is true when a woman is set apart to function as an officer or teacher in a Church organization under the direction of one who holds the keys of the priesthood. Whoever functions in an office or calling received from one who holds priesthood keys exercises priesthood authority in performing her or his assigned duties."[9]

If I'm understanding correctly, then, even young women set apart in presidencies of classes act with priesthood authority, as do women (and men and youth) in a wide variety of other assignments and callings. I assume this delegation of authority could happen in a variety of ways. For example, in addition to a man being ordained to the priesthood, men or women could be given priesthood authority by

- the laying on of hands when they are set apart to a calling;
- verbal or informal assignment, such as being assigned and authorized to minister to a family or individual;
- written authorization through a document (like a temple

---

9. Oaks, "The Keys and Authority of the Priesthood."

recommend needed to do baptisms for the dead or a certificate of one's status as a missionary);
- being endowed in the temple, as alluded to by President M. Russell Ballard: "Like faithful sisters in the past, you need to learn how to use the priesthood authority with which you have been endowed to obtain every eternal blessing that will be yours."[10]

In summary, Jesus Christ delegates priesthood authority to both men and women in His Church.

THE HOLY GHOST GIVES US GIFTS TO TUTOR US IN SPIRITUAL POWER

The influence and gifts of the Holy Ghost tutor us in the faith, humility, compassion, and vision that turn priesthood authority into priesthood power. Of course, getting priesthood power is not about paying my dues and fulfilling my part of a bargain that obligates God to give me a miracle. I don't get to see an angel, heal my sister, convert an investigator, or speak like Moroni each time I open my mouth just because I want to, or have good intentions, or pay my tithing, or even because I live a life of faith and sacrifice. While personal righteousness and practice with the gifts of the Spirit can help us qualify for spiritual power, we cannot simply earn our way to enough spiritual muscle to do whatever we want, independent of God. His is the power, and we will do no more than borrow it in this life, on His terms and according to His will, wisdom, and timing.

As we've already noted, powerlessness itself can actually prepare us for power by helping us learn humility, compassion, discipline, meekness, and other essential traits of Deity. The Lord reminds us that He gives us weakness that we may be humble, and that

---

10. M. Russell Ballard, "Women of Dedication, Faith, Determination, and Action," BYU Women's Conference address, May 1, 2015.

humility and faith in Him help us qualify for grace, which is His enabling power to make our experience with mortal weakness become empowering to us.[11]

BY OATH AND COVENANT, GOD HAS PROMISED ASTOUNDING BLESSINGS

As a result of the Atonement of Jesus Christ, the sanctifying power of the Holy Ghost, and our obedience and sacrifice, we can be born again. We can receive the image of God in our countenance and be changed from within. Eventually we can become enough like God in character to be filled with His glory and power.

This process is described by Joseph Smith in the *Lectures on Faith*: "All those who keep his commandments shall grow up from grace to grace, and become heirs of the heavenly kingdom, and joint heirs with Jesus Christ; possessing the same mind, being transformed into the same image or likeness, even the express image of him who fills all in all: being filled with the fulness of his glory, and become one in him, even as the Father, Son and Holy Spirit are one."[12]

These promises are reiterated in the oath and covenant of the priesthood described by the Lord in Doctrine and Covenants 84:33–40. Sister Linda K. Burton, as General President of the Relief Society, once invited the women of the Church to memorize these verses because "the blessings and promises of the oath and covenant of the priesthood pertain to both men and women."[13]

In those verses, we read: "For whoso is faithful unto the obtaining these two priesthoods of which I have spoken, and the magnifying their calling, are sanctified by the Spirit unto the renewing of their bodies. They become the sons of Moses and of Aaron and

---

11. See Ether 12:27; Bible Dictionary, "Grace."
12. *Lectures on Faith*, 5:2.
13. Linda K. Burton, "Priesthood Power—Available to All," *Ensign*, June 2014.

the seed of Abraham, and the church and kingdom, and the elect of God. And also all they who receive this priesthood receive me, saith the Lord; for he that receiveth my servants receiveth me; and he that receiveth me receiveth my Father; and he that receiveth my Father receiveth my Father's kingdom; therefore all that my Father hath shall be given unto him. And this is according to the oath and covenant which belongeth to the priesthood. Therefore, all those who receive the priesthood, receive this oath and covenant of my Father, which he cannot break, neither can it be moved."

We notice that our part of the covenant is only alluded to. But the Lord's covenant with us is exquisitely spelled out: If we receive and magnify priesthood authority and receive God's servants who have keys to administer it, we can receive Christ, His Father, His Father's kingdom, and all that His Father has.

How do women "obtain" these two priesthoods? The role of ordinances in this process, as explained and taught by Moses to his people, prefaces the verses above: "And this greater priesthood ["which is after the holiest order of God"] administereth the gospel and holdeth the key of the mysteries of the kingdom, even the key of the knowledge of God. Therefore, *in the ordinances thereof,* the power of godliness is manifest. And *without the ordinances thereof, and the authority of the priesthood,* the power of godliness is not manifest unto men in the flesh; for without this no man can see the face of God, even the Father, and live. . . . And the lesser priesthood . . . holdeth the key of the ministering of angels and the preparatory gospel" (D&C 84:18–22, 26; emphasis added).

President M. Russell Ballard (and President Joseph Fielding Smith) assure us that all these promised blessings and the pathway to them are not limited to men holding priesthood offices or keys: "When men and women go to the temple, they are both endowed with the same power, which by definition is priesthood power. While the authority of the priesthood is directed through priesthood keys, and priesthood keys are held only by worthy men, access to the power and blessings of the priesthood is available to all of God's children.

"As President Joseph Fielding Smith (1876–1972) explained: 'The blessings of the priesthood are not confined to men alone. These blessings are also poured out upon . . . all the faithful women of the Church. . . . The Lord offers to his daughters every spiritual gift and blessing that can be obtained by his sons' (Joseph Fielding Smith, "Magnifying Our Callings in the Priesthood," *Improvement Era*, June 1970, 66). . . .

"Our Father in Heaven is generous with His power. All men and all women have access to this power for help in their lives."[14]

In conclusion, our Father and Savior want to endow both men and women with power—endless power, Their power, the power to receive and eventually empower those we love with all that They have and are. The power of God is the power to do endless good for endless people over endless ages by supporting them in learning to do the same for successive generations of God's children. We are on earth to grow in that power, now.

---

14. M. Russell Ballard, "Men and Women and Priesthood Power," *Ensign*, September 2014.

Chapter 3

POWER FROM ON HIGH

And now, Holy Father, we ask thee . . . that all people who shall enter upon the threshold of the Lord's house may feel thy power, . . . And that they may grow up in thee, and receive a fulness of the Holy Ghost, and be organized according to thy laws, and be prepared to obtain every needful thing.

DOCTRINE AND COVENANTS 109:10, 13, 15
(DEDICATORY PRAYER FOR THE KIRTLAND TEMPLE)

In New Testament times, the resurrected Savior counseled His Apostles to tarry at Jerusalem until they were "endued with power from on high" (Luke 24:49), a directive He reiterated to His disciples in latter days when He commanded them to build a temple: "I gave unto you a commandment that you should build a house, in the which house I design to endow those whom I have chosen with power from on high; For this is the promise of the Father unto you; therefore I command you to tarry, even as mine apostles at Jerusalem" (D&C 95:8–9).

Having read these scriptures, when I first received the temple endowment I think I unconsciously expected to learn some secret to the universe that would give me power to change the world, or at least myself. Instead, years of exposure to the temple have shown me peace and perspective even when the world doesn't change, as well as the self-compassion and hope to try again when I don't either.

Along with fasting, prayer, and sacrifice, ordinances help us grow in spiritual power: "Therefore, in the ordinances [of the Melchizedek priesthood], the power of godliness is manifest" (D&C 84:20). Perhaps the ordinances of the temple help women in particular to grow in priesthood power; the temple is, after all, "the house of the daughters of Zion" (D&C 124:11). As referenced in the scripture at the start of this chapter, in the temple we can "grow up in [God]," we are "organized according to [God's] laws," we can "receive a fulness of the Holy Ghost," and we are "prepared to obtain every needful thing" our Father has to offer to help us fulfill our missions and accomplish His work of saving the human family. Let's explore a few of the ways the temple might specifically help women grow in priesthood power.

IN THE TEMPLE, WOMEN LEARN ABOUT CHRIST AND THEMSELVES THROUGH SYMBOLS

Temple ordinances teach us symbolically about who Christ is and who we are and can become. Women who often feel underrepresented in the scriptures may nevertheless see themselves in gospel symbols that compare Jesus Christ to women or teach gospel principles through women's experiences.

John A. Widtsoe, an Apostle from 1921 to 1952, taught, "We live in a world of symbols. No man or woman can come out of the temple endowed as he should be, unless he has seen, beyond the symbol, the mighty realities for which the symbols stand."[1] When I first read this statement as a teen I assumed it meant I should study

---

1. *Power from on high: Fourth year junior genealogical classes* (Salt Lake City: Genealogical Society of Utah, 1937).

the meaning of various scriptural symbols like numbers or colors or articles of clothing in order to understand the temple better. But I've since concluded that the "mighty realities" the Lord intends for us to have "seen" are much more than equations like the number ten equals perfection, or the color green equals life, or headdresses equal authority, or Adam equals humankind. I think those "mighty realities" are literal spiritual experiences, changes of heart and mind, and deepening relationships with God and His Son. As Christian writer C. S. Lewis suggests, "Symbolism exists precisely for the purpose of conveying to the imagination what the intellect is not ready for."[2] Even before we are prepared to fully grasp them, ordinances suggest images of these mighty realities to our imagination.

These are some of the mighty realities that symbols help us grasp as we try to deepen our connection with Deity:

- Being born again by choice and covenant into the family of the Father, Son, and Holy Ghost (see Moses 6:59).
- Adding to our personal identity the name of the Son of God (see 3 Nephi 27:5).
- Acquiring true spiritual protection impenetrable by the world (see Ephesians 6:11–16).
- Obtaining a level of faith that only comes through sacrifice (see *Lectures on Faith*, 6:5).
- Receiving a fullness of the Holy Ghost that prepares us to obtain every other needful thing (see D&C 109:15).
- Learning the language and work of angels (see 2 Nephi 31:13–14).
- Experiencing the presence of God (see Matthew 5:8).
- Being organized into eternal families (see Genesis 2:24).[3]

---

2. In Walter Hooper, ed., *The Collected Letters of C. S. Lewis, Vol. II* (San Francisco: Harper, 2004), 565.
3. See also, for example, William S. Harwell and Fred C. Collier, eds., *Manuscript History of Brigham Young, 1847–1850* (Salt Lake City: Collier's Publishing, 1997), 35.

- Being endowed with a portion of one of God's most identifying powers: the power to engender spiritual life and power in others (see D&C 132:19–20).

I feel wonder and awe as I contemplate the gospel symbols and ordinances that teach us about these things. These symbols and ordinances draw heavily on the lives of women and remind us that Christ, as the high priest for women as well as men, can "be touched with the feeling of our infirmities, [being] in all points tempted like as we are," including *as we are* as women (Hebrews 4:15).

When we're trying to unpack a spiritual symbol, we can start by asking what the symbol reminds us of, or what it is like. When you think of baptism, the sacrament, or ordinances of the temple, ask yourself what they are like. Do any of these come to mind?

- A midwife at the birth of a baby
- A parent feeding a meal to a family
- A parent washing and dressing a wound for a child
- A bride changing her name when she marries
- A mother dressing her daughter for her wedding
- A grandparent greeting a family member after a long absence

I can't help but notice how common these events are in the lives of women. They are not all *exclusively* female experiences, to be sure, but they are certainly *common* female experiences, and if we want to understand the mighty spiritual realities underlying gospel ordinances, being a woman may help. Consider the symbol of baptism. How is this like our mortal birth? Of course, we don't remember being born, so we don't have a lot of personal experience to draw on there. So let's go to the other side of the birth experience. What is birth like for a mother? For a midwife? Who is the mother and midwife of our new birth? The Savior.

When I was pregnant with our first child, my husband Dave

gave me a beautiful priesthood blessing. In it, he unexpectedly promised me that during this pregnancy I would gain special insight into the Atonement of Jesus Christ. Excited, I began studying scriptures about the Atonement in search of this insight. Nothing particular jumped out. I prayed fervently for help in knowing how to secure this blessing. *Nada.* I read a book about the Atonement. Interesting, but nothing new. Pregnancy rolled on. I didn't get any special insight into Christ's Atonement. I just got increasingly tired and uncomfortable.

And then I went into labor. I began to suffer. Despite the intellectual understanding I had from books about what labor and delivery would involve and how to relax and breathe my way through it, this was a whole new ballgame. I felt completely unprepared. I wondered how I would survive this process that took over my body. I bled. I cried out. I prayed. I longed for someone to help me, or at least to stay with me while I endured. I remember falling to my knees and crawling on the floor with the pain of transition. During delivery I broke out in a rash of little red dots across my face and torso from the pressure of pushing. A necessary sacrifice, one more painful than I had previously imagined, secured new life for someone I had not even met in this life. And I loved that person in ways I had never experienced before.

Oh. *That* kind of insight into the Atonement of Christ.

If we want to learn about baptism, our "new birth," we may get only as far as imagining a warm bath unless we think about what birth really is like for a woman in labor. Is there anything the Atonement of Christ is more "like" than labor, a woman's labor, bringing new life to an unborn child (see Isaiah 53:11)?[4]

Of course, men suffer too, deeply, and sometimes out of great personal sacrifice as they go to work or to war to feed or protect

---

4. Read about the Savior's Atonement in Matthew 26:37–42 and Doctrine and Covenants 19:18–19.

others. Those sacrifices should also be gratefully contemplated when we think of the Atonement. But if we want to learn what King Benjamin meant when he said we are both begotten and born of Christ, then the experience of women giving birth seems pretty important to consider since fathers beget and mothers give birth. King Benjamin says: "And now, because of the covenant which ye have made ye shall be called the children of Christ, his sons, and his daughters; for behold, this day he hath spiritually *begotten* you; for ye say that your hearts are changed through faith on his name; therefore, ye are *born of him* and have become his sons and his daughters" (Mosiah 5:7; emphasis added).

Baptism is like a birth, accomplished through the personal sacrifice and labor of a mother, and Christ is like that mother. But baptism is also different from a mortal birth, and those differences are also instructive. For starters, not all mothers must suffer in these particular ways. More crucially, the suffering and the impact of Christ's labor for us was far greater than a mortal can endure. Its impact was not only personal but also universal. It brings us not only mortal life but immortality and the potential for eternal life.

In a similar way, if we want to learn about the sacrament, we might consider a mother putting food on the table for her family, or nursing a baby, or taking a meal to the needy. The children eat at her table because they are her family, and we eat at Christ's table because we are His. In ancient Israel, the families of the priest and of the sacrificer who had brought an offering to the temple ate the parts of the sacrifice that were not burned up as an offering to God. We are the family of Christ, and He stands symbolically in all the roles of priest, sacrificer, and sacrificial offering for us (see Leviticus 7:11–18; 10:12–15). Christ feeds us spiritually like the king *or queen* who becomes a nursing father or a nursing mother to the scattered house of Israel (see Isaiah 49:22–23). In fact, a "nursing father" is a symbol for only a man who acts toward a child in a maternal, nurturing way, as does the Savior with us.

Other ordinances might make us think of the midwives who have swaddled countless generations, or our mothers putting ointment and white dressings on our bloody knees to comfort us and help us heal. We might remember the constant vigilance a parent almost instantly acquires for a vulnerable newborn and what that can teach us about the watchful and protective eye of a God who never forgets us (see Isaiah 49:15). The Aramaic word translated as *endued* or *endowed* means "clothed." In addition to thinking of a priest clothing himself in special garments before beginning his work in the ancient temple, might it also inform our understanding to think of a mother helping her daughter dress for her wedding, since we are all, female and male, part of the Church that is the bride of Christ? The English word *endow* comes from a Latin word, *dotare*, from *dos*, for "dowry." How is the endowment like a dowry given to a woman by her parents when she marries?

Women have tried for millennia to learn from scriptural stories that are primarily about men by imagining how the stories might also apply to us. But in contemplating some of our most important symbols, both women and men learn about Christ by thinking of Him as being like a mother (see Isaiah 66:13), or ourselves as being like His bride (see D&C 133:10, 19–20; Hosea 2:14–16). No symbol perfectly applies across the board, but these comparisons can help us learn about Christ as the Person behind the *mighty realities*—who He is, what He did for us, what He feels for us, and what He promises to make of us. These *mighty realities* are hinted at by the *ordinary realities* of women's lives as well as men's. I invite you to contemplate these images when you ask about a gospel or temple symbol, "What is it like?"

Taking this idea further, what other comparisons does Christ make to help us understand Him, His character, His feeling, and

His mission? To what does Christ liken Himself? Is He in some ways like the kindly Samaritan, the son of the lord of the vineyard, or the sower of seeds that fell in many place—all men in parables He shared? Absolutely. *And* He compares Himself to

- the *woman* who searches without ceasing until she finds her lost coin (see Luke 15:8–10);
- a *hen* gathering her chicks under her wings (see 3 Nephi 10:9–10);
- a *mistress* watching over her handmaidens (see Psalm 123:2);
- a *female* sheep being shorn (see Isaiah 53:7; Mosiah 14:7);
- a nursing *mother* (see Isaiah 49:15; 1 Nephi 21:15);
- a *woman* giving birth (see Isaiah 53:11; the word *travail*, also referring to a woman's labor in childbirth, as in Isaiah 54:1).

Christ's very name, *Jesus, Joshua, Yeshua,* means "God is help," like Eve was a "*help* meet for [fitting for] Adam" (Genesis 2:20; emphasis added). I'm told the only person other than Eve who is called a *help* with this same Old Testament word is God, Jehovah, who is our Help (see Psalm 33:20). Adam may have gotten to name all the animals, but latter-day revelation specifies that Eve is first named by God (see Moses 4:26). The name *Eve* is derived from the Hebrew words *chawah* and *chayah,* meaning "to breathe" or "to live." Her name means "life." Who else in the scriptures is called Life? Christ (see John 11:25). What might we learn from these comparisons?

We also note that biblical animal symbols for the Savior are often male animals, but they are not *only* male animals. The sacrificial lambs offered in the temple that symbolize *the* Sacrificial Lamb usually could be and sometimes had to be *female* (see Leviticus 3:1; 4:28; 5:6). The red heifer whose ashes cleansed people from sin and uncleanness was a perfect *female* cow (see Numbers 19:2–9). For Old Testament farmers and herdsmen, what would be the greater sacrifice, a male or a female animal? Female animals that could bear offspring were crucial to the growth of the herd, so sacrificing a female sheep or ox or cow was like burning up your seed corn, your capital, your most important asset normally to be protected at all costs. Male animals were more expendable because their role in enlarging the flock (how shall I put this?) was more limited. So given a choice, the ram got offered up before the ewe, and not just because his horns made better trophies. But in offering the very best to God, sometimes the greater sacrifice of a female was required.

Men also make great sacrifices. Throughout history, society has put men, not women, on the front lines, in factories and mines, on sailing ships and on crosses. I think of my sons and my grandsons and I hate that this is the case. It makes me weep to think of the sacrifices they may be called upon to make. Women increasingly share in these sacrifices today. In pointing these things out, I'm certainly not trying to imply that, in the eyes of God, men's lives matter any *less* than women's lives. But can we review all this and still wonder if God thinks men matter *more?*

These images help me see a broader image of who Jesus is—an image that includes both traditionally masculine and traditionally feminine traits. I'm grateful that female lives provide at least some of the images Christ draws on in explaining the mighty realities behind some of our most important symbols for who He is, and for how both He and we operate in the world with the holy and divine power to engender spiritual life in others (see Mosiah 15:10, 12–14). Godly men and women may develop this power in slightly different contexts, but we all have sacrifices to make and work to do and labors to perform to bring spiritual life to the world.

The symbols used to represent the Savior assure us that, though a man, He fully and physically understands the lived experience of women. In the words of Sister Chieko Okazaki, Counselor in a former Relief Society General Presidency: "We know that Jesus experienced the totality of mortal existence in Gethsemane. It's our faith that he experienced everything—absolutely everything. Sometimes we don't think through the implications of that belief. We talk in great generalities about the sins of all humankind. . . . But we don't experience pain in generalities. We experience it individually. That means he knows what it felt like when your mother died of cancer—how it was for your mother, how it still is for you. He knows what it felt like to lose the student body election. He knows that moment when the brakes locked and the car started to skid. He experienced the slave ship sailing from Ghana toward Virginia. He experienced the gas chambers at Dachau. He experienced Napalm in Vietnam. He knows about drug addiction and alcoholism.

"Let me go further. There is nothing you have experienced as a woman that he does not also know and recognize. On a profound level, he understands the hunger to hold your baby that sustains you through pregnancy. He understands both the physical pain of giving birth and the immense joy. He knows about PMS and cramps and menopause. He understands about rape and infertility and abortion. His last recorded words to his disciples were, 'And, lo, I am with you always, even unto the end of the world' (Matthew 28:20). He understands your mother-pain when your five-year-old leaves for kindergarten, when a bully picks on your fifth-grader, when your daughter calls to say that the new baby has Down syndrome. He knows your mother-rage when a trusted babysitter sexually abuses your two-year-old, when someone gives your thirteen-year-old drugs, when someone seduces your seventeen-year-old. He knows the pain you live with when you come home to a quiet apartment where the only children are visitors, when you hear that your former husband and his new wife were sealed in the temple last week, when your fiftieth wedding anniversary rolls around and your husband has been dead for two years. He knows all that. He's been there."[5]

I can feel myself drawing closer to the Savior in gratitude and wonder as I realize how intimate, how personal, His compassion is for me. One of His names really is Life. And all of His names really can be mine.

IN THE TEMPLE, WOMEN ARE AUTHORIZED BY JESUS CHRIST TO ENTER HIS ORDER

Christ authorizes His priesthood representatives, male and female, to convey ordinances and covenants in the temple. Thus women as well as men are "organized according to [His] laws" within His "holiest order" (D&C 109:15; 84:18). Stepping into priestly robes, roles, and covenants, women are authorized and prepared to perform temple ordinances on behalf of the dead.

The Melchizedek Priesthood was originally known as the "Holy Priesthood, [note the comma] after the Order of the Son of God" (D&C 107:3). We don't talk much about this order today, but Alma and others do, for it has existed from the beginning. This "holy order, which was after the order of his Son, . . . was from the foundation of the world; or in other words, [is] without beginning of days or end of years, being prepared from eternity to all eternity, according to his foreknowledge of all things" (Alma 13:1, 7). "This is the order after which [Alma was] called, yea, to preach unto . . . every one that dwelleth in the land . . . to cry unto them that they must repent and be born again" (Alma 5:49).

It seems to me that remnants of the idea of this order persist in many of the world's religions that have religious orders today. These orders are groups of people like monks or nuns who set themselves apart from society and take solemn vows to discipline their lives

---

5. Chieko Okazaki, *Lighten Up!* (Salt Lake City: Deseret Book, 1993), 174.

according to their understanding of the teachings of their founder. In a similar way, God wants us to be a people set apart from the world as a community of Saints, organizing ourselves according to the teachings and example of Jesus Christ. We're not trying to join the Order of Joseph Smith or the Order of Melchizedek, but to enter the Order of the Son of God. The Melchizedek Priesthood is organized "after" this order.

In a religious order, monks or nuns take vows to order their personal lives and show devotion to God, such as vows of obedience to superiors, of silence, of celibacy, or of poverty. It is interesting to think about the covenants and promises we make in the temple to govern our speech, our sexuality, our wealth, our dress, and our time in accordance with God's holy principles and laws.

Melchizedek is one who was specifically called as a priest after this holy order: "Melchizedek was ordained a priest after the order of the Son of God. . . . All those who are ordained unto this priesthood are made like unto the Son of God" (Joseph Smith Translation, Hebrews 7:3).

"And men having this faith, coming up unto this order of God, were translated and taken up into heaven. And now, Melchizedek was a priest of this order; therefore he obtained peace in Salem, and was called the Prince of peace. And his people wrought righteousness, and obtained heaven" (Joseph Smith Translation, Genesis 14:32–34).

We note that *Melchizedek* means "king of righteousness," and he was the prince of *Salem* (which means "peace"). Many others were also called to this order (see Alma 13:1–20), but no wonder the Priesthood after the Order of the Son of God is called after a king of righteousness who was the prince of Peace (see D&C 107:3).

However, formal bearers of the priesthood are not the only ones who enter the order. In President Ezra Taft Benson's stunning article, "What I Hope You Will Teach Your Children about the Temple," we read more about this order, which President Benson says both Adam and Eve entered, and which we as their sons and daughters may enter today in the temple: "When our Heavenly Father placed Adam and Eve on this earth, He did so with the purpose in mind of teaching them how to regain His presence. . . . Adam and his posterity were commanded by God to be baptized, to receive the Holy Ghost, and to enter into the order of the Son of God.

"To enter into the order of the Son of God is the equivalent today of entering into the fullness of the Melchizedek Priesthood, which is only received in the house of the Lord.

"Because Adam and Eve had complied with these requirements, God said to [each of] them, 'Thou art after the order of him who was without beginning of days or end of years, from all eternity to all eternity' (Moses 6:67)."

President Benson then refers to Adam gathering his righteous posterity in the valley of Adam-ondi-Ahman to give them his last blessing, adding: "The Prophet Joseph Smith said that Adam blessed his posterity because 'he wanted to bring them into the presence of God' (*Teachings of the Prophet Joseph Smith*, sel. Joseph Fielding Smith [Salt Lake City: Deseret Book, 1938], 159). . . .

"How did Adam bring his descendants into the presence of the Lord? By entering into the priesthood order of God. Today we would say they went to the house of the Lord and received their blessings.

"The order of priesthood spoken of in the scriptures is sometimes referred to as the patriarchal order because it came down from father to son.

"But this order is otherwise described in modern revelation as an order of family government where a man and woman enter into a covenant with God—just as did Adam and Eve—to be sealed for eternity, to have posterity, and to do the will and work of God throughout their mortality. . . .

"Adam followed this order and brought his posterity into the presence of God. . . .

"Moses taught this order of priesthood to his people and 'sought diligently to sanctify his people that they might behold the face of God; But they hardened their hearts and could not endure his presence' (D&C 84:23–24). . . .

"The Lord further instructed Moses, 'I will take away the priesthood out of their midst; *therefore my holy order,* and the ordinances thereof' (Joseph Smith Translation, Ex. 34:1).

"My purpose in citing this background is to illustrate that this order of priesthood has been on the earth since the beginning, and it is the only means by which we can one day see the face of God and live (see D&C 84:22). . . .

"Even though the Aaronic Priesthood and Melchizedek Priesthood had been restored to the earth, the Lord urged the Saints to build a temple to receive the keys by which this order of priesthood could be administered on the earth again. . . . '*even the fulness of the priesthood*' (D&C 124:28). . . .

"When our children . . . go to the temple to receive their blessings . . . they enter into the same *order of the priesthood* that God instituted in the very beginning with father Adam."[6]

Entering this order is not enough to endow us with power, however. Alma explains the importance of righteousness if we are to live up to our privileges: "Now, as I said concerning the holy order, or this high priesthood, there were many who were ordained and became high priests of God; and it was on account of their exceeding faith and repentance, and their righteousness before God,

---

6. "What I Hope You Will Teach Your Children about the Temple," *Temples of the Church of Jesus Christ of Latter-day Saints,* 1988, 42–45; all italics added by Ezra Taft Benson.

they *choosing to repent and work righteousness* rather than to perish; Therefore they were called after this holy order, and were sanctified, and their garments were washed white through the blood of the Lamb" (Alma 13:10–11; emphasis added).

Today, in the dispensation of the fullness of times, both women and men are "called [into] this holy order," this priesthood order. We are vested in priestly robes and roles as were Aaron and his sons (see Exodus 29:4–9) to perform ordinances on behalf of the dead for whom we officiate in initiatory, endowment, and sealing rooms. Within these priestly roles, we may be further authorized as temple workers to also perform ordinances for the living.

IN THE TEMPLE, GOD SHOWS WOMEN THE BLESSINGS OF THE OATH AND COVENANT OF THE PRIESTHOOD

In addition to forms of power we might begin to emulate here, Christ is also described as having power we can't fathom: power over every creature in heaven, in the earth, and in the sea (see Revelation 5:13); power to receive all riches, wisdom, strength, honor, glory, and blessings (see Revelation 5:12); power over all His enemies, including death (see 1 Corinthians 15:25–26); power over all rule and authority of this earth (see 1 Corinthians 15:24) and over all the powers, principalities, dominions, and names of this world and the world to come (see Ephesians 1:21); power to govern as the head of His Church (see Ephesians 1:22); power to reveal the secrets of His will (see D&C 76:24); power to do anything He takes in His heart to do (see Abraham 3:17); and power to empower those who receive Him to become the sons and daughters of God (see John 1:12; 2 Corinthians 6:18; Mosiah 5:7).

Men and women who become His sons and His daughters through faith on His name and submission to His will, His teachings, and His priesthood order will eventually share in all these powers as we become "heirs alongside Jesus Christ of all our Father has."[7] As President Dallin H. Oaks reminds us, "The purpose of The Church of Jesus Christ of Latter-day Saints is to help all of the children of God understand their potential and achieve their highest destiny. Our theology begins with heavenly parents. Our highest aspiration is to be like them."[8]

From whom do you stand to inherit something? From a celebrity you've never met? A billionaire who finds your name by chance on the internet? A stranger who wants to pass a cherished family estate in Somalia to someone who loves water buffalo farming? Not so much. We inherit from people who love us and claim us as family. We inherit from people who are pretty sure we actually want what they want to give us. Most importantly, perhaps, we inherit from people who trust us not to use our inheritance to destroy ourselves or others. That means those who pass on their material assets to us must also pass on the skills, stories, character, and values that will help us manage them wisely.

Likewise, we become trustworthy with all God wishes to give us when we learn to love what He loves, live as He lives, and serve whom He serves. And God loves, lives for, and spends His eternal life on relationships. The oath and covenant of the priesthood is not just a promissory note for assets or truths or health or even virtues God will one day give us. It is an offer to be in a relationship—to receive Him, His family, and ours. President Henry B. Eyring affirms, "We can picture ourselves home again with our Heavenly Parents in that wonderful place, not only as sons and daughters but husbands and wives, fathers and mothers, grandfathers and grandmothers, grandsons and granddaughters, bound together in loving families."[9]

As a recipient of that promise, Moroni, the last Nephite standing

---

7. M. Russell Ballard, "Men and Women and Priesthood Power," *Ensign*, September 2014.
8. Dallin H. Oaks, "Apostasy and Restoration," *Ensign*, May 1995, 84.
9. Henry B. Eyring, "The Family," *Ensign*, February 1998.

in the Book of Mormon, still lived out his final days enfolded in a circle of relationships. He was awed by the story of the brother of Jared, who had preceded him by thousands of years. He saw his future readers and fretted about what they would think of his "weak" words. He took comfort in the reassurance that Jesus Christ had prepared a place in heaven for him and for all the truly charitable: "I have seen Jesus, and . . . he talked with me face to face, and that he told me in plain humility, even as a man telleth another in mine own language, concerning these things" (Ether 12:39). Moroni sent messages of hope and instruction to future generations, reverently assuring us that we will one day "see [him] at the bar of God" (Moroni 10:27). Moroni's lonely life was still meaningful, powerful, because of God's assurance that his words would make it to our ears.

Understanding of such covenant relationships in the kingdom of God is precisely what was lost with the Apostasy: "This 'falling away' does not represent some minor corruptions of sacramental liturgy or ritual forms. It is not about wicked priests whom God punished by removing their priesthood. It is about a fundamental misapprehension of the background and purpose and extent of the covenant . . . [and] the mode by which that covenant is executed. . . .

"The loss was not about baptizing at the wrong age or in the wrong medium. It was about not knowing that baptism makes us—all of us eventually—literally members of Christ's family and co-heirs with him as planned in premortal councils. What is at stake is not simple difference in standards of sexual practice of marriage's purpose per se. It is about failing to see the family structure as a divine mode of eternal association that is at the very heart of heaven itself. . . . . In Joseph's understanding, the tragedy that befell Christendom resulted from a critically impoverished account of the everlasting covenant, one that rendered all sacraments and ordinances ineffectual not through wickedness but through lost understanding of their scope and purpose—namely to constitute the human family into a *durable, eternal, heavenly association.*"[10]

Within this holy order of the priesthood, God's covenant family of daughters and sons is organized and empowered. Brigham Young was shown something of this "durable, eternal, heavenly association" by Joseph Smith in a dream: "Joseph stepped toward me, and looking very earnestly, yet pleasantly said, 'Be sure to tell the people to keep the *Spirit of the Lord;* and if they will, they will find themselves just as they were organized by our Father in Heaven before they came into the world. Our Father in Heaven organized the human family, but they are all disorganized and in great confusion.'

"Joseph then showed me the pattern, how they were in the beginning. This I cannot describe, but I saw it, and saw that the Priesthood had been taken from the earth and how it must be joined together, so that there would be a perfect chain from Father Adam to his latest posterity."[11]

When we exercise our agency to order our lives after our covenants and keep the Spirit of the Lord, we will be organized into joyous, healthy, loving, covenant relationships with God and with one another. In eternity, the righteous can have both roots and branches in that grand design, even if here we have neither. This is the essence of eternal *Life*.

---

10. Fiona and Terryl Givens, *The Christ Who Heals: How God Restored the Truth that Saves Us* (Salt Lake City: Deseret Book, 2017), 14–15; emphasis added.
11. William S. Harwell and Fred C. Collier, eds., *Manuscript History of Brigham Young*, 35; emphasis in original.

Part 2

PRIESTHOOD POWER THROUGH ANCIENT AND MODERN PRIESTHOOD RESPONSIBILITIES

In this section we will consider how women and men, operating under priesthood authority, participate in various ways in the responsibilities and opportunities scripturally associated with each office in the Aaronic or Melchizedek Priesthood. It might feel like a stretch to suggest, as I am about to, that Christ feeding the five thousand was acting in a deacon's role, and that a woman taking food to a soup kitchen or feeding her family might be too. It might likewise feel like a stretch to suggest that in praying for the health of a friend, a woman can access the same prophetic gifts as an elder giving a priesthood blessing. In exploring such ways of thinking, my goal is neither to dilute the importance of priesthood offices nor to imply that women already do everything priesthood holders do.

Rather, I hope to throw light on the ways women's lives and experiences inform a lot of what the priesthood is doing in the first place, and to spark our imagination about how ordinary acts can be infused with holiness and power. I hope to clarify the ways priesthood work is women's work as well as men's work, priesthood privileges women's privileges as well as men's privileges. I hope to help us liken the work of the priesthood unto ourselves as women, the way we liken the scriptures unto ourselves even when they talk about men. I hope that in the process, women and men can begin to imagine many more ways to feel more empowered to participate creatively in God's work with His blessing and to His glory.

Chapter 4

NOURISH ZION

DEACON

It is wise to fear that our own skills are inadequate to meet the charge we have to nourish.... But that realistic view of our limitations creates a humility which can lead to dependence on the Spirit and thus to power.

HENRY B. EYRING

After the death and Resurrection of Jesus Christ, the Church was initially centered in Jerusalem among people who had seen and known the Lord. They included both local Jews who had grown up around Jerusalem and spoke Aramaic and Hebrew, and recent immigrants who, even though they had a Jewish heritage, had grown up in Greek cities with Greek cultures and speaking Greek.

All these early converts, Hebrew and Greek alike, apparently came together daily to share communally-held food. But all was not well in their little Zion. The Greek immigrants noticed that their widows were being "neglected in the daily ministration" that was presumably supervised by the locals (Acts 6:1). They brought this inequity to the Apostles' attention.

The Apostles counseled with all the members about this problem (in what language, I don't know!), and they all concluded that it didn't make sense for the Twelve to neglect their teaching and

> **DUTIES OF THE OFFICE OF DEACON**
> - Assist teachers (D&C 20:57)
> - "Watch over the church, [and] be standing ministers unto the church" (D&C 84:111)
> - "Warn, expound, exhort, and teach, and invite all to come unto Christ" (D&C 20:59)

missionary commissions to "serve tables" (Acts 6:2). So the Twelve asked the Church members to choose seven good men to make sure the food was distributed fairly. Those chosen, who all had Greek names, interestingly enough, were called the Seven (not very imaginative, but it stuck). These men were set apart by the Twelve (I see a trend here) to minister to these temporal needs of the early Saints (see Acts 6:1–6). The word for their primary duty—to "serve" or "wait on" tables—is the Greek word *diakonos*, from which the noun *deacon* also comes—a word that means something like waiter or servant.

This story intrigues me for a couple of reasons. First, it reminds me that the titles associated with various priesthood functions (e.g. Levite, deacon, teacher, Seven, Twelve) were not written in the sky. Other than the word *priest*, they were common words that could apply to lots of people (such as daughters of Levi or seven sisters). Later they were used as names of priesthood offices. That's helpful to me as a woman. Even though I don't hold priesthood offices, I have often been set apart to similar responsibilities or informally filled similar roles. For example, anyone can be called and set apart as a teacher in the Church, and even class members who are not called sometimes teach me as much as the formal teacher does. I can also study and develop the characteristics implied by these once-common words, such as being fair, wise, humble, or a student of the scriptures.

Second, this story makes me wonder if there is something important about serving food that I need to understand. In the Church today, serving the sacramental meal is the role of deacons (it has always been a priesthood role, but not always a deacon's role[1]). Is there something important, even priestly, about feeding people, whether literally or symbolically? Serving food is something I've done a lot of, but it doesn't usually seem especially holy. In fact, it is generally noisy and messy. But if priesthood holders act in the name of Christ and with His authority, did Christ or His Apostles also act in deacon-like roles? Are there ways women can draw on priesthood power as we nourish others? Is priesthood power needed by women and men to nourish people, to distribute the resources of a community fairly, or to truly meet the needs of the poor? I believe the answer to all of these questions is *yes*. Before we look at how, let's review briefly some additional historical context.

DEACON HISTORY

While priesthood power is eternal, those who hold the priesthood have functioned differently in different periods of mortal time. Adam held some form of priesthood from the time he left Eden, and he eventually attained the Melchizedek Priesthood (though it was not called that at the time) and passed it to his children (see D&C 84:16–17). So did Noah, Abraham, and others.[2] But beginning at the time of Moses, the higher laws of God were rejected by the people, and only a lesser priesthood and law continued (see D&C 84:25–26). In the entire house of Israel, and in the entire world, for that matter, only the tribe of Levi held even this lesser priesthood, and only the sons of Aaron within that tribe were actually priests (see Numbers 3:9–10).

Some of the priesthood roles of the Levitical (or Aaronic)

---

1. See William G. Hartley, "From Men to Boys: LDS Aaronic Priesthood Offices, 1829–1996," *Journal of Mormon History*, *Vol. 22*, No. 1, 83.
2. See Doctrine and Covenants 84:14 and notes on Facsimile 2 and 3 in the book of Abraham.

Priesthood became obsolete when the law of Moses was fulfilled in Christ. For example, animal sacrifices and offerings, which had been the mainstay of temple worship, were no longer required after the great and last sacrifice of the Savior (see Alma 34:13). So what happened to the priesthood once these sacrifices were no longer needed and as Christianity grew? The Apostles, although charged with the leadership of Christ's Church, did not have a right to this Levitical Priesthood, as they were not of the tribe of Levi. Nor, ironically, was Jesus, so He did not hold the Aaronic Priesthood by birthright: "For he of whom these things are spoken pertaineth to another tribe, of which no man gave attendance at the altar. For it is evident that our Lord sprang out of Juda; of which tribe Moses spake nothing concerning priesthood" (Hebrews 7:13–14).

Jesus Christ did hold, and was in a sense the author of, the higher Melchizedek Priesthood, or the Priesthood after the Order of the Son of God, which encompasses all other priesthood roles and responsibilities (see Hebrews 6:20; D&C 107:2–4). Christ ordained His Apostles to this higher priesthood, giving them authority to carry on the work of His Church after His death (see John 15:16). As the new Church grew in size, geography, and complexity, new priesthood roles and offices developed. The role of deacon was apparently among these (see 1 Timothy 3:8–13).

When the Church was restored in our day, priesthood offices associated with the Aaronic Priesthood were initially given to adult men, not youth.[3] The current structure of giving young men the Aaronic Priesthood beginning at age twelve and advancing them in office by age gradually took hold between 1908 and 1922 and was not completely institutionalized with the current ages of advancement until the 1950s. Eventually home teaching formally became a Melchizedek Priesthood responsibility instead of an Aaronic

---

[3]. For a thorough review of the history I've summarized in this section, see William G. Hartley, "From Men to Boys," 78–134.

Priesthood responsibility, as initially assigned. Aaronic Priesthood quorums were organized within wards instead of stakes. Lists of useful things for Aaronic Priesthood holders to do were circulated and slowly adapted to the capacity of young boys instead of mature men.

Young deacons and priests were not generally involved with administering or passing the sacrament until the 1880s and beyond. Some of the other responsibilities they were given were mundane things like chopping wood for fires, cleaning the chapel, leading the music, or other tasks that do not require any priesthood authority. Some were responsibilities that had previously been commonly assumed by women, young women, or even custodians, such as cleaning the sacrament cups and trays, washing and folding the linens, providing the bread, and laying out the bread and water on trays at the sacrament table before services.[4]

I review this history to remind us that not all of the roles and responsibilities associated with priesthood offices today are mandated scripturally. They have changed over time with changing circumstances and may change again. Even descriptions of these offices in the Doctrine and Covenants were originally directed to older men and may be applied differently today.

For many years in The Church of Jesus Christ of Latter-day Saints, the priesthood office of deacon has been conferred upon young men beginning at age twelve (although it hasn't always worked this way[5]). The most visible responsibility of these deacons today is to serve the sacrament to the members of a ward or branch each Sunday. Their scripturally appointed duty does not specify this assignment, however. They are simply to "assist" those with

---

4. See William G. Hartley, "From Men to Boys," 78–134.
5. In the early days of the restored Church, deacons were primarily adult men. Once the Saints settled in Utah, that trend continued, with younger boys gradually moving into their ranks. By the early 1900s, every young man from age twelve and up was expected to receive the Aaronic Priesthood, although the duties associated with that priesthood continued to be performed by adult men until much later.

other priesthood offices and "watch over the church" as "ministers" (D&C 84:111).

Under the law of Moses, the families of the priests were to eat the meat from the sacrificial animals along with bread and other non-meat offerings "in a clean place" (Leviticus 10:14). In a similar way, men, women, and children gather at the table of Jesus Christ and partake of the emblems of His sacrifice as members of His family. In other words, we might still think of the deacons as being those charged with distributing a meal to the Saints, only now it is a meal with a different meaning and purpose than the food distributed by either the Levitical priests or by the Seven. In a sense, the deacons stand in Christ's stead in distributing the food to all who are seated around His table, making sure no worthy members or guests are "neglected" in that ministration or distribution, regardless of their marital status or what language they speak or where they grew up. We can well imagine that if Christ attended a sacrament meeting today, He could take any of these roles of preparing, blessing, distributing, or partaking of the sacrament. We can imagine this because He already has demonstrated His willingness to prepare, bless, distribute, and partake of food in many settings. He instituted the sacrament both by blessing, distributing, and partaking of the food as He gave the Passover meal new meaning for His followers (see Mark 14:22–25; see also the Joseph Smith Translation), and by creating a new ritual moment around feeding the Nephites and Lamanites to whom He appeared after His Resurrection (see 3 Nephi 18:1–12).

There seems to be something important, even godly, about distributing food, serving the temporal needs of other people, and giving food a sacred role in the building of communities and of holiness. Certainly these are roles that women have played throughout human history as they nurse babies, feed families, take meals to the sick and bereaved, take up the responsibility of distributing the food of the bishop's warehouse, contribute to philanthropic efforts in the Church and elsewhere, and pass along the sacrament trays to those seated next to them.

THE GODLY ROLE OF DISTRIBUTING FOOD

In the beginning, God Himself assumed the responsibility of feeding humankind. When I think about it, this is, after all, what a good Parent does. In the Genesis account of the Creation, right after God blesses the newly created man and woman, commands them to multiply, and gives them dominion over every living thing, He tells them what's for dinner: "Every herb . . . and every tree . . . to you it shall be for meat" (Genesis 1:29). God plants a garden for Adam and Eve (think about that statement for a minute to contemplate the humility and meekness of God) and fills it with "every tree that is pleasant to the sight, and good for food," including the tree of life (Genesis 2:9). Satan wastes no time trying to usurp God's self-appointed role of feeding His children, however, enticing them with the one and only food God has warned them will be deadly.

The history of God's dealings with His people is colored by His role of distributing, and sometimes withholding, food. For killing his brother, Cain is cursed that the ground will not yield her strength when he tries to till the soil (see Genesis 4:12), but Jacob describes the God of his fathers, Abraham and Isaac, as "the God which fed me all my life long unto this day" (Genesis 48:15). God likewise feeds the new nation of Israel for forty years with manna from heaven as a symbol of His watchful care. God frequently chastens His people with famine, but He sends ravens to feed the prophet Elijah and then makes a nearly empty barrel of meal and cruse of oil sufficient to feed him and a faithful widow and her son until the rains come again (see 1 Kings 17:4, 14). He reproves Israel in a time of sin because "the shepherds [of Israel] fed themselves, and fed not my flock," so He steps in, promising to search out the lost sheep Himself and "feed them in a good pasture, and upon the high mountains of Israel . . . I will feed my flock" (Ezekiel 34:8, 14–15).

I'm not an especially good cook, and figuring out how to feed children who each had different favorite and untouchable foods drove me crazy at times. But I remember a friend telling of a time when she prayed to know what she should focus on that would bless her and her family spiritually. She felt she should pay more attention to ensuring that meals were healthy, happy experiences. It had never crossed her mind to see feeding kids as something of spiritual significance, but there seems to be something important, even godlike, about men and women distributing the earth's resources to feed God's children. When a foster child stops hoarding food in the backpack he keeps by his bed, foster parents realize the security and love they are providing is healing his body and soul. Once bishop's storehouses and humanitarian services and Relief Society sisters help meet people's physical needs, those people begin to notice their spiritual hungers and value spiritual nourishment.

That said, I'm not suggesting women be relegated to the kitchen any more than deacons should be relegated there. There are many important ways for women and men to feed the hungry, including the spiritually hungry. I'm grateful for the reminder, however, that even my meager efforts to eat nutritiously, feed my children, be hospitable to guests, or write a check to the food bank are not only physically but spiritually relevant (and grateful to know that deacon is not the only priesthood office to be emulated!).

CHRIST AS DEACON

Jesus Christ, the Jehovah of the Old Testament who provides manna to the Israelites, retains His flock-feeding role during His mortality. In fact, Jesus teaches that He is the Bread of Life that comes down from heaven that, unlike manna of old, will completely satisfy the hunger of those who eat it, giving them eternal life (see John 6:48–50). Christ further demonstrates His role as the Shepherd and feeder of the flock when, on two occasions, He feeds thousands of people with a few loaves and fishes (see Mark 6:30–42; 8:1–9; John 6:5–13).

Consider the ironic setting for one of these occasions: Christ proposes taking His Apostles to the desert to "rest a while; for there were many coming and going, and *they had no leisure so much as to eat*" (Mark 6:31; emphasis added). Despite His efforts to feed them, however, the private, leisurely picnic is overrun with thousands of people eager to hear from this new and inspiring teacher. Rather than being annoyed, Jesus "was moved with compassion toward them, because they were as sheep not having a shepherd: and he began to teach them" (v. 34). Then, when the day is far spent, the compassion of the faithful Shepherd and Priest moves Him to feed His flock. There is not a bakery in sight; in fact, many bakeries would be woefully inadequate for such a crowd. But Jesus takes a little bread and fish, looks up to heaven to give thanks, breaks the loaves, and asks His disciples to take the deacon's role of distributing the miraculously multiplying food until more than five thousand "did all eat, and were filled" (v. 42).[6]

Christ had refused to feed Himself through supernatural means after fasting for forty days in the wilderness (see Matthew 4:4), but He does not hesitate to pull out all the stops in miraculously (and publicly) feeding His sheep. In this time period, men did the planting and harvesting and women prepared the food for

---

6. Even before His formal ministry begins, Christ miraculously (and privately) turns about 135 *gallons* of water into wine at the end of a marriage feast, just because his mother was worried they might run out. I don't know how many people typically showed up at the average wedding feast in Cana, but by any conceivable estimate that must have made for quite a feast (see John 2:1–10; a firkin was about nine gallons).

the family. But Jesus does it all from a few borrowed loaves and fishes as the disciples "wait on" the guests.

Even though there are thousands, millions, billions of us, Christ continues to feed us, too. As utterly unlikely as it seems, a woman could conceivably forget her nursing child, Christ teaches, but He will never forget us, engraven as we are on the palms of His hands (see Isaiah 49:15–16). He *feeds us* primarily, however, *through us*—through giving the basket of food over to us to distribute to the world. Both women and men share in this physical and spiritual commission. When we distribute the world's resources in accordance with His principles, there is enough and to spare (see D&C 104:17), for we are acting with godly power in a godly role.

At a Time Out for Women event, accomplished violinist Jenny Oaks Baker told of a particularly stressful time in her life when women in her ward brought a meal to her and her family. Jenny had been insistent that they didn't need the food, thinking it was unnecessary to burden others when she was perfectly capable of calling Domino's Pizza. But the women came anyway, not only bringing a meal but bringing helping hands, listening ears, and cheerful hearts. Jenny told the audience she realized that Domino's might have been more efficient at delivering pizza, but Domino's didn't deliver love.

Nourishing others physically and spiritually is fundamental to the roles of priesthood bearers, and of women organized within priesthood patterns, orders, and authority. As President Henry B. Eyring reminds us in an early conference talk, quoted at the beginning of this chapter, we need the power of the Holy Ghost if we are to discharge this duty with inspiration, effectiveness . . . and power.

When at the time of the Fall, Eve was enabled thereby to bear and nurse children and Adam was charged to eat bread by the sweat of his brow, their tutoring in the holy role of feeding God's family began. This time they had to plant their own garden, learning to till fields, distinguish weeds from herbs, domesticate animals, tend flocks, and teach all these things to their children (see Moses 5:1–3). I can vividly imagine Eve experiencing the process of nourishing unborn children in her womb but also having to figure out the sometimes complicated task of nursing babies, and finding food they would eat, and figuring out what's for dinner, and teaching the family to participate in feeding themselves, and helping her daughters and sons repeat these processes through multiple generations. I suspect that none of this was easy, given that it is not easy for me. But it probably taught them all a variety of skills such as patience, curiosity, learning from setbacks, service, discipline, attention to detail, and enjoying the moment.

It also certainly taught them some of the attributes of godliness we'll consider next: gratitude, eyes to see and ears to hear, relationship building, and empowering others.

SKILLS AND ATTRIBUTES OF PRIESTHOOD POWER: GRATITUDE

Let's face it: most of you reading this book probably have the skills and resources to put food on your table. In fact, you may have more than enough to eat, which can be its own problem. But stop for a moment and think about all the people whose labor you depend on to plant, grow, weed, harvest, transport, prepare, package, sell, and clean up after every item of food you don't personally grow. Even if you have a garden, who provided you with the seeds, the hose, the hoe, the gloves, the cookpot, the stove, the sink, the table? Consider the giant web of industry and skill that supports your fragile life. Who farmed, watered, harvested, baked, packaged, transported, invented, marketed, stocked, or sold all these resources that make your life work?

I will never forget a sacrament meeting prayer given by a new member of our ward as she humbly recognized, thanked God for, and asked God's blessings on all those laborers, listing them as if they were in the room with us. I was poignantly reminded of how many thousands of people I blindly rely on to bring food to my little table each day. My gratitude and humility deepened. I began to wonder: Am I grateful for what I have? Am I doing my part to equitably distribute the food God prepared the earth to bring forth to all who hunger and thirst? How can I better express appreciation to those who are?

SKILLS AND ATTRIBUTES OF PRIESTHOOD POWER: EYES TO SEE AND EARS TO HEAR

Like good deacons, we need to "watch over the church" as "ministers" (D&C 84:111). When distributing the temporal and spiritual resources of the Church to all, we especially need eyes to see and ears to hear those we are trying to feed. Jehovah chastised ancient Israel for being a "foolish people, and without understanding; which have eyes, and see not; which have ears, and hear not" (Jeremiah 5:21). Jesus specifically chastised His disciples when they didn't understand and remember His power to feed them, saying: "Having eyes, see ye not? and having ears, hear ye not? and do ye not remember? When I brake the five loaves among five thousand, how many baskets full of fragments took ye up? They say unto him, Twelve. And when the seven among four thousand, how many baskets full of fragments took ye up? And they said, Seven. And he said unto them, How is it that ye do not understand?" (Mark 8:18–21).

In our day He invites the "ignorant [to] learn wisdom by humbling himself and calling upon the Lord his God, that his eyes may be opened that he may see, and his ears opened that he may hear" (D&C 136:32).

When I watch the deacons in my ward pass the sacrament, I notice how they are trained by their service to see in a new way, paying attention to things they haven't had to think about before. They have to see where their fellow deacons are going, notice the empty rows, remember the people in the foyer, and track how much is left on the tray. They have to learn to see anew, including putting themselves in the shoes of the person with the broken arm, the woman with three small children, the four-year-old who wants to "do it himself" but can't quite manage, the visitors who aren't sure what is happening, the person who got skipped, and the person who doesn't partake.

Perhaps the most touching demonstration I've seen of a deacon learning to see with new eyes occurred when a young man in my ward I'll call Jason, who has Down syndrome, passed the sacrament for the first time. I know his parents and advisers had worked carefully to prepare Jason for this new responsibility, which he very much wanted to assume. But they did more than prepare *him*. They prepared his whole quorum. The quorum members were prepared to not only watch over Jason but to be Jason's eyes as he learned to watch over his new "flock" of ward members waiting to be fed.

It looked like this: That particular Sunday, and each Sunday thereafter for many weeks, one of his fellow twelve-year-old quorum members stood at Jason's side as he carried out his duties. Jason's companion did not hold a tray but gently guided Jason row by row, pointing out where he needed to go next, helping him solve problems that arose, and smiling with encouragement as Jason learned to see the pattern of how to pass the sacrament so all could receive it. I'm sure the deacon helping Jason learn to see was himself learning to see with fresh eyes as well—to see the needs of his quorum brother, the love of his parents, and images of humility and of power. All in the congregation were learning to see these things too. I still tear up remembering those images.

When I really stop to see and hear, I also note that women participate in many ways in this sacramental meal. Let's consider a few.

The responsibility has been given to the deacons to make sure neither widows nor anyone else is neglected in this distribution, but everyone in the congregation, including women, helps the deacons fulfill this duty. The weekly sight of the tray in our hands can become a signal, a reminder to bring our minds back to both the Savior in whose name we are served and our brothers and sisters at His table who we make sure also receive. The privilege of serving the sacrament is substantial, but far overshadowed by the privilege of receiving it and sharing it.[7]

I remember the Sunday a member of our bishopric thanked the members of the Aaronic Priesthood and the young women in the ward for providing the sacrament for us that day. There were a lot of confused looks until he added that the young women had decided to learn to bake bread so they could provide the bread for the sacrament each week. Many a woman has included on her shopping list bread for her son to take to church to be laid out, broken, and distributed by young men holding the priesthood.

Women do not just listen to the priestly prayer but may join the "we" whose desires are voiced in it as "we" sing and pray in the name of Christ, "O God, the Eternal Father, who dwells amid the skies, *in Jesus' name we ask thee* to bless and sanctify, if we are pure before thee, this bread and cup of wine, *that we may all remember that offering divine*" (*Hymns*, no. 175; emphasis added). While the ordinance is clearly performed by the priest at the table,[8] we can all say "amen" to the prayer.

---

7. According to Hartley, the deacons' role in passing the sacrament was a fairly late development not mandated in the scriptures, and President Heber J. Grant once indicated to a mission president that holding the priesthood was not a prerequisite for passing the sacrament, since everyone in the congregation assists with this task.
8. This was demonstrated for me when I attended a ward of primarily hearing-impaired members. The priests at the sacrament table gave the prayer in sign language, while the woman translating the meeting for hearing members spoke orally the words of the prayer. Although she said the words aloud, there was no question that the sacrament was being blessed under the authority of the priests' priesthood.

The Saints in Jerusalem who chose the Seven also learned to see anew. The Hebrew speakers among them had their own style and expectations for distributing the food, and apparently they didn't even notice the Greek widows were being neglected. I'm not sure what was going on there. Maybe the Hebrews saw olives as a delicacy that no one should get more than one of, but the Greeks normally ate olives as a staple. Or maybe the Greek widows didn't even come to the distribution because they were expected to stay home in mourning, and the Hebrews didn't know who they were well enough to notice their absence. Or maybe the widows were just lashing out about their lonely plight with unrelated complaints. It doesn't matter: the group saw the problem, including the problem with putting the Apostles in charge of passing out the food to the neglect of weightier duties. These Saints wanted so much to correct this lapse, rather than defend or justify it, that *once they saw,* they chose seven *Greeks* who would see with different eyes to be in charge of the food.

Problems with distributing food are not always so easily resolved. Sometimes well-meaning people set up service projects or try to minister to others without adequately consulting those they are trying to help. The helpers may come away from the project feeling good about the food they gave out, the advice they gave, the garden they planted, or a lesson they taught, but those "helped" may feel mostly patronized or invisible.[9] As a close-to-home example, a sister in my ward recently shared a time when her daughter, who had just moved to a distant city, called her in tears.

"What happened?" the mother asked.

"My visiting teachers just dropped off brownies for my birthday," her daughter reported.

"So why the tears?"

---

9. See Robert D. Lupton, *Toxic Charity: How Churches and Charities Hurt Those They Help, and How to Reverse It* (New York: Harper One, 2012).

"I just wish they had invited me to make the brownies with them instead. I don't need brownies, but I really need friends."

It takes time and care to develop eyes to see and ears to hear those we are trying to serve. We truly are ignorant when we start out, but as we humbly call on the Lord, ask more questions, observe more carefully, let those we are trying to serve teach us about their needs, listen to their suggestions, and especially as we seek and hearken to the voice of the Spirit, we gain eyes and ears to see and hear with compassion and wisdom how we can best fulfill our deacon-like role of distributing the food, and all the earth's resources, to the physically and spiritually hungry.

SKILLS AND ATTRIBUTES OF PRIESTHOOD POWER: RELATIONSHIP BUILDING

A third set of skills and attributes we need in order to administer our priesthood-assigned duties with power has to do with building relationships. One of the most frequent and time-honored ways of building community is through shared meals. When we celebrate family events, we do it with food. It wouldn't be a ward activity without refreshments. Most of us don't need the calories, but we are starving for belonging. Just as Christ nurtured relationships and created lasting memories with His disciples and friends as He ate with them, families and communities create relationships and memories as they share food, conversation, and prayers with loving intent.

Now, let's face it: every meal isn't Thanksgiving dinner. At some meals there is laughter and delight, thoughtful expressions of gratitude for God and for one another, meaningful teaching moments, and mutual involvement in the preparation and cleanup as skills are passed to the next generation. At others there is more tension, silence, complaining, or insistence that one or another is being "neglected in the daily ministration"—especially the daily ministration of dessert! But with practice we can learn to share relationships, not just calories, as shared meals become opportunities to minister to our loved ones with godly power, compassion, gratitude, and delight. We can listen for the heartache hidden in complaints or silence, ask questions with genuine curiosity and compassion instead of implied criticism, and build the communities that will one day become Zion.

It can certainly feel like it is hardly worth the time to put a meal together when McDonald's can do the job in 46 seconds, nor do we always feel up to competing with Wolfgang Puck, Julia Child, or our mother-in-law in the kitchen. As a result, the simple community-building acts of family meals or having people over for dinner have dwindled in recent decades—at least at my house. But I clearly cannot afford to give up on these age-old rituals. For openers, inviting our former missionaries over for "game night" and food once a month after my husband and I returned from our mission resulted in one of our former sister missionaries showing up at our door. She and our son, also visiting, hit it off. They are now expecting our ninth grandchild!

Also, when our daughter moved to a new ward as a mid-single, she knew she would need to make an effort to meet friends. The ward she was assigned to had lots of older singles and couples, but she noticed only one single woman who looked about her age. She invited her to dinner. They had a good conversation, so they decided to do it again the next week and see who else they could find to join them. Those weekly dinners continued for years, eventually growing to twenty or thirty participants each week. My daughter was eventually blessed with lifelong friendships and a husband as a result. (And we got two grandchildren. Are you seeing a trend?)

I've seen so many ways people have built community and belonging by sharing food and resources with others. Instead of just going out to lunch, one relative of ours regularly involves her friends and her young children in preparing and serving soup and bread for a local Ronald McDonald House. A single friend doing foster care learned that her own eating habits improved when she had to put food on the table regularly for someone else. A Relief Society president we know organized a garden that ward families worked in together and mutually benefited from. At the start of each year, some friends with ample resources fund a special checking account they then prayerfully distribute to individuals and charitable causes; their Christmas gift to each other is reading together the list of individuals and groups who have benefited from their efforts. A Primary president we love recently invited some of her Primary girls and their school friends over for a movie and popcorn, strengthening bonds among the Primary girls and their friends of other beliefs.

Someone who created community simply by having people over regularly for food admonishes: "The number of real friendships you'll create is related to . . . how many intimate experiences you create. To create experiences, you have to schedule them. You have to prioritize them . . . understanding that these experiences can deliver what you want—a group of friends who would stand together in tough times, enjoy the calm times, and celebrate the happy times . . . collecting skills, wisdom, access, money, and strength that can be found only in community."[10]

SKILLS AND ATTRIBUTES OF PRIESTHOOD POWER: FROM EMPOWERED TO EMPOWERING

A final quality of priesthood power is that it empowers us and others. We may not think of waiting tables as either powerful or empowering, but when the Savior of the world is the waiter, our perception might change.

---

10. Charles H. Vogl, *The Art of Community: Seven Principles for Belonging* (Oakland, California: Berrett-Koehler Publishing, 2016), 158.

On the shore of Galilee, the resurrected Christ again takes the humble role of a deacon, hosting His closest friends for dinner. From the lakeshore He calls to His disciples, fishermen in their boats, "Children, have ye any meat?" (John 21:5). When they call back to this apparent stranger that they've caught nothing, He tells them where the elusive fish can be found. They only recognize Him when the catch is too abundant to be explained by anything other than His miraculous gift.

Then, in light of our discussion about the godly role of feeding others, imagine this scene: the risen Savior stooping in the dirt to build a fire, tend to the coals, knead the bread, clean the fish, and invite His friends to the "intimate experience" of sharing His fire: "As soon then as they were come to land, they saw a fire of coals there, and fish laid thereon, and bread. . . . Jesus saith unto them, Come and dine. And none of the disciples durst ask him, Who art thou? knowing that it was the Lord. Jesus then cometh, and taketh bread, and giveth them, and fish likewise. . . . So when they had dined, Jesus saith to Simon Peter, Simon, son of Jonas, lovest thou me more than these? He saith unto him, Yea, Lord; thou knowest that I love thee. He saith unto him, Feed my lambs. . . . Feed my sheep" (John 21:9, 12–13, 15–16).

This is just bread and fish, the simple meal of simple men, but it seems to be Jesus's "signature" dish. Today's equivalent would be something like hamburgers or soup from the grocery store. He is not creating a gourmet meal; He is creating an experience of connection and caring.

In this scene we also see a pattern for conveying godly power. Christ first lends His disciples His power to find the fish, and then they draw on their own skills to bring in the catch. They then come to the warmth and bounty of His fire to be nourished physically and spiritually. Finally, He extends a commission to pick up His work: "Feed my lambs, my sheep."

PRIESTHOOD POWER THROUGH PRIESTHOOD RESPONSIBILITIES

Peter passes this commission later to those early converts, perhaps including those who struggled to make sure the widows were fed. He encourages them to first be nourished with the mother's milk of God's word, and then, in their deacon-like roles, to feed the flock of the God who has fed and cared for them: "Wherefore laying aside all malice, and all guile, and hypocrisies, and envies, and all evil speakings, As newborn babes, desire the sincere milk of the word, that ye may grow thereby: . . . Feed the flock of God which is among you, taking the oversight thereof, not by constraint, but willingly; not for filthy lucre, but of a ready mind; Neither as being lords over God's heritage, but being ensamples to the flock. . . . Casting all your care upon him; for he careth for you" (1 Peter 2:1–2; 5:2–3, 7).

Christ asks, and then promises: "Who then is a faithful and wise servant, whom his lord hath made ruler over his household, to give them meat in due season? Blessed is that servant, whom his lord when he cometh shall find so doing. Verily I say unto you, That he shall make him ruler over all his goods" (Matthew 24:45–47).

There is spiritual power—priesthood power—hidden in the simple acts of coming to the fire of Christ as the family and disciples of the Father's Deacon, receiving at His hand, and then turning our hands outward to distribute the bread and water to a congregation, a family, a nation, a world.

There are countless ways for us to pick up this divine commission to nourish and empower others, depending on our circumstances, callings, skills, and interests. When we do so prayerfully and thoughtfully, we are promised the approbation, and power, of heaven: "That a feast of fat things might be prepared for the poor; yea, a feast of fat things, of wine on the lees well refined, that the earth may know that the mouths of the prophets shall not fail; Yea, a supper of the house of the Lord, well prepared, unto which all nations shall be invited. First, the rich and the learned, the wise and the noble; And after that cometh the day of my power; then shall the poor, the lame, and the blind, and the deaf, come in unto the marriage of the Lamb, and partake of the supper of the Lord, prepared for the great day to come. Behold, I, the Lord, have spoken it" (D&C 58:8–12).

Chapter 5

BUILD COMMUNITY AND BELONGING
TEACHER

By union of feeling we obtain pow'r with God.

Joseph Smith, speaking to the Nauvoo Relief Society

We are all teachers. We teach with words and stories, and we teach with actions and attitudes. We teach family members, friends, coworkers, and neighbors in a thousand informal interactions and as ministers, missionaries, temple workers, presidents, librarians, clerks, and camp directors. And we teach as teachers.

As I first thought about how women especially might participate in the power of the priesthood office of a teacher, I felt reassured. How hard could this be? After all, I've seen plenty of examples of women teaching, and teaching well. I could draw on personal experience as a teacher in a wide variety of settings. There are a lot of teachers in my family, so thinking and talking about teaching is an everyday occurrence at our house. The scriptures would give me a lot to ponder about teaching, too.

Then I read exactly what the Doctrine and Covenants says about the priesthood office of teacher, and I went from reassurance to panic. As those verses sunk in, I realized the duties of the office of a teacher didn't have a lot to do with teaching at all, in the traditional sense. They had to do with something I was *not* sure I'd seen good examples of, *didn't* have a lot of experience with, *hadn't* read or talked much about, and had only recently even *started* pondering. Specifically, it looked like the priesthood power to be found in the office of teacher has to do with crafting community and building belonging. It is less about classrooms and more about family rooms, chat rooms, neighborhood barbecues, ward campouts, showing up for funerals, and showing up for dinner. It begins and ends with relationship.

> **DUTIES OF THE OFFICE OF TEACHER**
>
> - "Watch over the church always, and be with and strengthen them" (D&C 20:53)
> - "See that there is no iniquity in the church, neither hardness with each other, neither lying, backbiting, nor evil speaking" (v. 54)
> - "See that the church meet together often, and also see that all the members do their duty (v. 55)
> - "Warn, expound, exhort, and teach, and invite all to come unto Christ" (v. 59)

Wendy, the community builder? Not quite. (In fact, I just came home early from our ward's 4th of July pancake breakfast to sit by myself at a computer all day rewriting this chapter . . . on building community!) But there is an old saying: When the student is ready, the teacher will come. Maybe the priesthood office of a teacher can be my teacher, and yours, in the priesthood power of creating community and building belonging.

THE PRIESTHOOD OFFICE OF TEACHER

I note that in the description of all the priesthood offices in section 20 of the Doctrine and Covenants (written shortly after the Church was organized in 1830), the duties listed for *every* priesthood office include at least a few synonyms for teaching—words like *exhort, preach, expound, warn,* and *invite—and* every single priesthood office is specifically called to *teach.*

Ironically, however, the office of a teacher focuses mostly on . . . something else. As listed above, the teacher's specific duty is to "watch over the church always, and be with and strengthen them." Teachers are to see that people don't sin, lie, backbite, or speak evil of one another, aren't hard with one another, and meet together often (D&C 20:53–55). Apparently teaching with priesthood power is not just about teaching per se, but about watching out for people, standing by them, hearing them, strengthening them, and encouraging them. If we're looking for how this office might teach us about priesthood power, then it will apparently be the kind of power referenced by Joseph Smith at the start of this chapter, power that comes through unity.

This is the power of kindness, talking things through without "hardness," defensiveness, "lying," or "backbiting;" encouraging people to simply keep coming to meetings, and when they don't, figuring out why and fixing it if possible. This is the power of loving people whether or not they come to meetings, in fact; looking on the heart and not external appearances. Ironically, the words of Joseph Smith's mother, Lucy Mack Smith, to the early Relief Society sisters could not provide a more apt summary of the principles inherent in the work of an Aaronic Priesthood teacher: "We must cherish one another, watch over one another, comfort one another, and gain instruction that we may all sit down in heaven together."[1]

How can women and men live up to our privileges of the priesthood power of creating community and building belonging?

TEACHING AND COMMUNITY IN THE PRIMITIVE CHURCH

Both teaching per se and aspects of the teacher's role that focus on community building are relevant to our understanding of the role of an Aaronic Priesthood teacher and its application to women.

---

1. In Relief Society Minute Book, Nauvoo, Illinois, March 24, 1842, 18–19.

Teaching itself has always been central to the gospel, and the office and role of teacher have evolved over millennia. A rabbi, which means a teacher, was an important leader in a Jewish religious community at the time of the Savior's mortal life.[2] Rabbis studied the scriptures in great depth so they could teach and counsel people on fine points of the law of Moses, and also so they could help the people get along. Priests ran the temple, but rabbis led the community. In some time periods and among some Jews, rabbis have been ordained by the laying on of hands by another rabbi so ordained who could attest to the recipients' training and experience. Some rabbis still try to trace their authority back to Moses, who ordained Joshua by the laying on of hands. Moroni specifies how "priests and teachers" were ordained in the Church that Christ established in the Book of Mormon (Moroni 3:1, 4). Perhaps related to this long tradition, "teacher" is an office in the priesthood today.

Jesus was known as a wise and powerful teacher, even by many who did not accept His divinity. He did not have a legal earthly right to the Priesthood of Aaron, but He was recognized as a rabbi whose deep scriptural understanding prepared Him to teach (see Matthew 7:28–29; John 3:2). Christ was also called *Master*, a translation of either the Greek word *didaskalos*, which means teacher, or the Greek *kurios*, meaning one who has power or authority (Matthew 23:8; Luke 20:21). Mary Magdalene called Him *Rabboni* (John 20:16), a term usually reserved for a great master teacher or head of the Sanhedrin, the religious governing body of biblical Judaism.

We have no record of Christ being formally ordained as a rabbi by mortal hands. We do know that Christ's teaching was accompanied by great spiritual power. Nicodemus, a Jewish ruler, said to Jesus, "Rabbi, we know that thou art a teacher come from God: for no man can do these miracles that thou doest, except God be with him"

---

2. The word *rabbi* does not appear in the Old Testament.

(John 3:2). The people at Capernaum "were astonished at his doctrine: for his word was with power" (Luke 4:32). After the Sermon on the Mount, they were likewise "astonished . . . For he taught them as one having authority, and not as the scribes" (Matthew 7:28–29). Even the skeptics "were astonished, and said, Whence hath this man this wisdom, and these mighty works?" (Matthew 13:54). The two disciples who walked and talked with the resurrected Savior on the road to Emmaus, without recognizing Him at first, later said, "Did not our heart burn within us, while he talked with us by the way, and while he opened to us the scriptures?" (Luke 24:32).

One of the Savior's most powerful teaching moments took place during a prayer offered for the people He visited in the Americas after His Resurrection. They record: "The eye hath never seen, neither hath the ear heard, . . . and no tongue can speak, neither can there be written by any man, neither can the hearts of men conceive so great and marvelous things as we both saw and heard Jesus speak; and no one can conceive of the joy which filled our souls at the time we heard him pray for us unto the Father" (3 Nephi 17:16–17).

Whether in or out of the Church, there are teachers, and then there are "teacher[s] come from God."

According to Paul, the office of teacher and other priesthood offices are established in Christ's Church for a number of purposes, including: "For the *perfecting* of the saints, for the work of the *ministry,* for the *edifying* of the body of Christ: Till we all come in the *unity* of the faith, and of the *knowledge* of the Son of God [not knowing information *about* Jesus, but *knowing* Jesus], unto a perfect man, unto the measure of the stature of the fulness of Christ: That we henceforth be no more children, tossed to and fro, and carried about with every wind of doctrine, . . . But *speaking the truth in love,* may *grow up into him* in all things, which is the head, even Christ (Ephesians 4:12–15; emphasis added).

Here we see again that the purpose of gospel teaching is not just imparting information. The purpose is creating Saints and bringing them to unity of the faith, and, by *speaking the truth in love*, helping them develop a spiritually mature relationship with one another and with Jesus Christ (see Mosiah 18:8–10). As psychologist Carrie Skarda puts it, "Part of the promise we are making at baptism is not just to God, but to each other. God isn't just forming a covenant person, but a covenant people. We are to become a Zion *people,* not a Zion *person.*"[3]

It is humbling to ponder in any relationship interaction, "What am I teaching right now? What is this person learning from me? Am I teaching indifference, impatience, cynicism, or distrust? Or am I curious, edifying, trustworthy, and empowering? Am I *speaking the truth in love* in ways that help others grow up in Christ?"

THE PRIESTHOOD ROLE OF TEACHER

As with the role of deacons described in the last chapter, how an Aaronic Priesthood teacher's duties are carried out (and by whom) has changed even over the last 200 years. In the early days of The Church of Jesus Christ of Latter-day Saints, only adult men held the Aaronic Priesthood offices. Only later, in Utah, was the Aaronic Priesthood given primarily to adolescents. However, much of the work of teachers was not really considered appropriate for adolescents to do, so Melchizedek Priesthood holders were formally called as "acting teachers" to fulfill those responsibilities, which included all sorts of community-building efforts—visiting all the families in a given block of a city, ministering to their needs, adjudicating disputes, assessing the adequacy of repentance, recommending Church discipline for the unrepentant, assisting the poor, and in general performing many functions handled today by bishops—*not teaching*.[4]

---

3. Personal correspondence.
4. See William G. Hartley, "From Men to Boys: LDS Aaronic Priesthood Offices, 1829–1996," *Journal of Mormon History, Vol. 22,* No. 1 (1996), 83.

The role of block teachers eventually morphed into ward teachers and visiting teachers, and then home teachers, and then, most recently, ministering brothers and sisters. "Ministering is Christlike caring for others and helping meet their spiritual and temporal needs."[5]

When teenagers came to predominate in the Aaronic Priesthood quorums, they accompanied Melchizedek Priesthood holders as apprentices in fulfilling these sacred, mature duties of watching over, being with, and strengthening the Church community. Leaders also suggested a variety of other "useful" but not scripturally mandated tasks suited to young men, such as collecting fast offerings, conducting music, setting up the sacrament trays (a task that had commonly been performed by building custodians and sometimes women), and making sure meetinghouses were clean, cared for, and warm for meetings (no small task in the days of wood-burning stoves).[6] This history reminds us that there has been more flexibility in how the Church and the priesthood operate than we sometimes realize—and that it takes a lot of sometimes unglamorous work to build a community.

Of course, teaching itself is also crucial in the Church. The word *teach* is from the Old English verb *taecan*, meaning to show or explain. *Teach* is also related to the Old English noun *tacen*, or *token*, referring to a sign, symbol, or evidence. Thus we might say

---

5. Letter from the First Presidency, dated April 2, 2018, https://www.lds.org/mycalling/ministering/first-presidency-letter?lang=eng.
6. See Hartley, "From Men to Boys." Harley notes that another reason for bringing younger boys into the Aaronic Priesthood was a growing concern in the mid- to late 1800s that these young men, though sons and grandsons of pioneers, were not necessarily well schooled in the gospel or well prepared for adult responsibilities in the kingdom. There were many reports of young men engaged in roughhousing, gangs, swearing, violations of the Word of Wisdom, breaking the Sabbath, defacing Church property, and getting into many kinds of mischief (just as there was concern that the young women were becoming too enamored with worldly dress and habits). The Sunday School, Primary, and Young Women's and Young Men's Mutual Improvement Associations were organized to help remedy these ills. Ordaining younger men to the Aaronic Priesthood was another part of the remedy.

that to *teach* the gospel with authority and power is to explain or point out the signs, symbols, tokens, or evidence of God's work in the world and His plans for us here. Other verbs listed with the priesthood office of a teacher in Doctrine and Covenants 20:53–59 and Moroni 3:3 include *exhort* (to encourage or strongly urge), *expound* (to present or explain something systematically and in detail, especially scriptures or doctrine), *warn* (to inform people in advance of impending danger), *invite* (to formally request that someone participate or act), and *preach* (to deliver a religious sermon, proclaim doctrine, or advocate moral behavior).

These are strong words, and each an important part of gospel teaching. If we preach and expound but don't invite or warn, we may be missing ways to access spiritual power as a priesthood-authorized teacher. We note that Emma Smith, first President of the Relief Society, was also "ordained" (we would probably say today "set apart" or "called") to "*expound* scriptures, and to *exhort* the church, according as it shall be given thee by my Spirit" (D&C 25:7; emphasis added).

We can also learn about obtaining power in our more formal teaching roles from the sons of Mosiah in the Book of Mormon, who "had given themselves to much *prayer, and fasting;* therefore they had the spirit of prophecy, and the spirit of revelation, and when they taught, they taught with *power and authority* of God" (Alma 17:3; emphasis added). The Lord also counsels teachers to "first seek to *obtain my word,* and then shall your tongue be loosed; then, if you desire, you shall have my Spirit and my word, yea, the *power of God* unto the convincing of men" (D&C 11:21; emphasis added).

UNHALLOWED TEACHING AND COMMUNITY

In contrast to teachers with priesthood power, Jesus Christ told Joseph Smith in the Sacred Grove that the religious teachers or professors of his day "draw near to me with their lips, but their hearts are far from me, they *teach* for doctrines the commandments of men, having a form of godliness, but they deny the *power* thereof (Joseph Smith—History 1:19; emphasis added). False teachers lead people away from true and saving principles and often build competing communities that undermine faith: "But there were false prophets also among the people, even as there shall be false teachers among you, who privily shall bring in damnable heresies, even denying the Lord that bought them, and bring upon themselves swift destruction" (2 Peter 2:1).

After periods of personal confusion or of widespread rebellion or adversity, however, faithful teachers can bring us back to the covenant path: "And though the Lord give you the bread of adversity, and the water of affliction, yet shall not thy teachers be removed into a corner any more, but thine eyes shall see thy teachers: And thine ears shall hear a word behind thee, saying, This is the way, walk ye in it, when ye turn to the right hand, and when ye turn to the left" (Isaiah 30:20–21).

With our own deep preparation and the help of heaven, we can be among the teachers, human and divine, who whisper direction and comfort to God's children, helping them back into fellowship and community.

"STUDENT TEACHERS"

Many times, students themselves become the teachers. Priesthood holders attending the School of the Prophets in Kirtland learned that the roles of teacher and student are interchangeable: "Appoint among yourselves a teacher, and let not all be spokesmen at once; but let one speak at a time and let all listen unto his sayings, that when all have spoken that all may be edified of all, and that every man may have an equal privilege" (D&C 88:122).

In a similar way, the sisters of the Nauvoo Relief Society counseled together to solve problems and strengthen one another in council settings we are using again today to build community: "Councillor [Elizabeth Ann] Whitney . . . invited all present to speak their sentiments freely. . . . The meeting was very interesting, nearly all present arose & spoke, and the spirit of the Lord like a purifying stream, refreshed every heart."[7]

Just as the effectiveness of the sacrament is facilitated by, but not dependent on, the spiritual power the priests bring to the ordinance, the effectiveness of gospel teaching is facilitated by, but not limited to, the spiritual power of the teacher. Mature students take responsibility for their learning and growth.

Elder Richard G. Scott taught this principle powerfully. He was once a student in the class of a humble teacher whose love for his students and pure intent allowed great spiritual strength to attend his teaching, even though he was not sophisticated in the gospel. In this atmosphere, because Elder Scott had made "prolonged, prayerful efforts to learn," important spiritual impressions came to him about his assignments in that area. These he recorded and acted on, changing the course of his life.

Another time, Elder Scott had a teacher who might have been a powerful teacher in a worldly sense but who was not a spiritually empowering or unifying teacher. Nevertheless, Elder Scott as a student was prepared to be taught by the Spirit, so he was. Even in this less than spiritual environment, he says: "I received such an outpouring of impressions that were so personal that I felt it was not appropriate to record them in the midst of a Sunday School class. I sought a more private location, where I continued to write the feelings that flooded into my mind and heart as faithfully as possible. After each powerful impression was recorded, I pondered the feelings I had received to determine if I had accurately expressed them in writing. As

---

7. Relief Society Minute Book, April 19, 1842, 31, 33; http://www.josephsmithpapers.org/paper-summary/nauvoo-relief-society-minute-book/30.

a result, I made a few minor changes to what had been written. Then I studied their meaning and application in my own life.

". . . . I was then impressed to ask, 'Was there yet more to be given?' I received further impressions, and the process of writing down the impressions, pondering, and praying for confirmation was repeated. Again I was prompted to ask, 'Is there more I should know?' And there was. I . . . received some of the most precious, specific, personal direction one could hope to obtain in this life. Had I not responded to the first impressions and recorded them, I would not have received the last, most precious guidance."[8]

Elder Scott did five crucial things as a student in the classroom of a gospel teacher, even one who was not especially well prepared spiritually:

- He made "prolonged, prayerful efforts to learn."
- He wrote down the impressions that came to him.
- He pondered how to express his impressions accurately.
- He asked the Lord if he had gotten it all right.
- He asked if there was anything more.

These steps in spiritual revelation and communication have blessed my life as well. I have continued to reflect on them often for years, wondering how I as either a student or a teacher might facilitate such moments.

By watching wise women in my ward, I have also learned that students can do a lot to contribute to the learning and spirit of an entire class. In a Relief Society council I attended recently, the topic was how to talk to our children about the gospel. I was tired, cranky about this new format, and frankly checked out. But near the end of our council, my sleepy stupor was pierced by the clear voice of a sister sitting a few chairs away from me in the circle. As she started to speak, I felt something important was happening. I saw others perk

---

8. Richard G. Scott, "To Acquire Spiritual Guidance," *Ensign*, November 2009.

up as well. She reminded us passionately but clearly that powerful teaching moments within our families and communities do not only happen when we have prepared a great lesson or are reproving with sharpness. Powerful teaching moments happen most often, and perhaps most meaningfully, when walking to the grocery store with a grandchild, moving the chairs into the cultural hall, corralling the nursery children, or packing the car for Scout camp. This was the scripture she shared, one her visiting teacher had shared years before with her: "And these words, which I command thee this day, shall be in thine heart: And thou shalt teach them diligently unto thy children, and shalt talk of them when thou sittest in thine house, and when thou walkest by the way, and when thou liest down, and when thou risest up" (Deuteronomy 6:6–7).

POWERFUL TEACHING AND EMPOWERING TEACHING

There are many techniques and tools of good teaching. Sometimes powerful teachers might impress us with their personal charisma, knowledge, experience, captivating stories, entertaining examples, provocative questions, and ability to stir deep feelings. Jesus Christ was a powerful teacher in all of these ways and more. But Christ was more than a powerful teacher. He was an empowering, unifying, community-building teacher. He empowered people to find new answers to their deepest questions about God, life, and themselves. He unified people to forgive, connect with, and relate to others. He empowered people to heal and grow to become not just more like Him, but more like their truest selves. He unified them with strength and commitment to do all these things for others, extending His reach across the globe and over two millennia—so far. When priesthood power accompanies our teaching, we too can be unifying and empowering, not just entertaining and wowing.

In the chart below I try to capture some of the differences between a powerful teacher and an empowering, unifying, community-building teacher. Remember that Christ excelled at all of the skills in both columns, and drew all of these reactions from others (even the negative ones). So may we.

Powerful Teachers	Empowering and Unifying Teachers
Purpose	
Pass on what they know and demonstrate personal power.	Help students figure out what they need to know and help them learn it.
Preparation	
Study and prepare lessons, become good storytellers and presenters, plan ways to grab and hold attention, and get people involved.	Study the gospel and seek the Spirit through fasting and prayer; plan ways to help students explore their values and overcome real obstacles in living them.
Relationship Assumptions	
Appreciate that having students gives the teacher an opportunity to learn, grow, and develop personal strengths.	Recognize that students and teachers give one another an opportunity to learn together and from the Spirit to develop strengths that strengthen others.
Methods	
Prepare great presentations, tell interesting personal stories, create great visual aids, use humor and drama, demonstrate expertise, keep attention, give assignments, and challenge thinking.	Create learning experiences, listen as much as ask questions, help students develop frameworks for understanding and living the gospel, encourage pondering and self-reflection, create ways to deliberately practice the hard parts of living gospel principles, facilitate "a-ha" moments when the Spirit can teach and testify, and practice skills of charity and covenant relationships.

Powerful Teachers	Empowering and Unifying Teachers
Outcomes	
Students replicate the teacher's ideas, have positive impressions of the teacher, and feel motivated or inspired. Students may also fear or envy the teacher, feel motivated without knowing quite how to take action, or feel hesitant to admit ignorance or confusion.	Students develop their own ideas and increase their skills, feel safe sharing concerns or questions, get clearer about their own values, learn resilience in the face of obstacles, and find meaning and hope in the process. Students may feel gratitude for the teacher, but they also feel more connected with others and with the Spirit.

In short, powerful teachers may impress us and connect us with them (and that can be important in drawing us in), but empowering and unifying teachers connect us with ourselves, with one another, and with heaven. Such teachers build belonging and create community.

Perhaps the best example of both powerful and empowering teaching is Christ's visit to the Americas.[9] All the left-column power is there, but also all of the right-column power of loving, empowering, and building community. He not only taught people His doctrine but gave them experiences with Him and with one another that were so powerfully converting as to help them pass His teachings down to the next generations for hundreds of years. How did He do this?

I have studied Christ's visit not just in terms of what He taught, but how. I notice that He shared not only His doctrine but His scars, His food, His tears, His prayers, and His blessings. Each of those words represents a profoundly personal encounter with the

---

9. See 3 Nephi 9–26.

mind, body, heart, and soul of the real person of Jesus Christ. He united them with not only Himself but with one another, sending them out to gather and bring in others. He gave them a priesthood infrastructure, modeling for them how to use that priesthood to heal, bless, and feed one another physically and spiritually. He noticed when they were tired or confused and sent them to their homes to ponder and prepare, presumably both in solitude and in poignant family conversations. He demonstrated powerfully that He understood and deeply shared what mattered most to them: their wounded and their children. He promised again and again to return.

I have contemplated these chapters countless times trying to learn how I too might not only teach doctrine but build communities: layers of genuine intimacy and connection that would sustain deep personal conversion through successive generations for *hundreds of years*. Such practices are worth contemplating as we try to imagine how we, as Christ's disciples, can develop the spiritual power embodied in the duties of the priesthood office of a teacher who will "watch over, be with, and strengthen" the people of the Lord.

BUILDING OUR TOLERANCE FOR CLOSENESS

I should note, however, that when I read 3 Nephi, even though I feel a deep yearning to know the Savior as these people did, I also realize that I'm not sure how well I would tolerate this level of intimacy. To do so requires hanging on for an intense, soul-searching, weakness-exposing ride. It requires a level of vulnerability we don't get much practice with. It requires openness to being seen and known more deeply than most of us have the stomach for. It requires tolerance for deep feelings, including both heartache and joy, that people can't even describe in words. It also requires deep honesty that takes us out of our private bubbles and into the light of more genuine connection.

When I think of the moments in life that give me practice with such experiences, I think of women nursing babies and tending to elderly parents. I think of men in foxholes. I think of childbirth (now *there's* a moment of intensity, vulnerability, and exposure!). I think of marriage in its most intimate disagreements and connections. I think of discussing a misunderstanding with a friend and getting to forgiveness even when we never quite get to unity. I'm personally not very comfortable with sustained emotional intimacy of the kind described in 3 Nephi. But there are moments in my life as a woman, as a human, that may be training me to try. I wonder if I am showing up for them as often as I could.

Adversity plays an interesting role in building community. Tragedy can bring communities together, but individual tragedies often leave us feeling isolated, invisible, and disconnected. I guess there is nowhere to hide when we are all in a tragedy together. We don't just pretend we're fine. Neither do we feel the shaming voice in our heads that says others have been spared in ways we were not. Maybe there is more we can do to quiet that voice even in the absence of communal sorrow so community can grow in peace as well.

FINDING OUR LOVE

What might love for those we teach, or shared moments of intimacy, look like in settings a little less dramatic than heavenly beings descending from the sky?

I will never forget the temple president in Montreal, Quebec, who, speaking at a fireside, said he hadn't really believed speakers who said, "I love each and every one of you." He would think to himself, "You don't even know me, so you certainly can't love me." But as he sat looking at us, he felt the Lord's love for us, and it became his own. He realized that even though he did not know all of our names or circumstances, he knew how we felt when we read the Book of Mormon; he knew how much we loved our children; he knew how hard we tried to live the gospel. Knowing these things about us, he knew the most important things about us. And he loved us. I felt that he did love us (*I loved us!*), and I believed God loved us. I was ready to listen and learn from this great and good man.

I'll admit, it doesn't come naturally to me to make small talk with class members or strangers before I step into a teaching role. I'd rather sit in the corner and invisibly review my notes. But it is usually more important for me to prepare to love than to prepare to speak. I can touch that love as I ask even a few people about their week or what they are hoping for that day. When I do, it is easier for me to feel safe and connected and easier for others to ask hard questions, be real, get help, and feel deeply.

Perhaps my favorite example of someone finding her love for a stranger, someone she wanted to bring into community, is from the wife of Elder L. Tom Perry. Sister Perry hadn't been assigned as a teacher and did not hold that office, but she stepped up to the privilege of "being with," "watching over," and "strengthening" another: "On one Sunday, Sister Virginia Perry, whose husband L. Tom Perry was [then] president of the Boston Stake, noticed a woman who had quietly found a space on the back row in the Weston chapel, having arrived a few minutes late for sacrament meeting. She was wearing jeans and a T-shirt and had come on her motorcycle. Sister Perry quickly sensed that the woman felt that she didn't fit in. Everyone else was wearing their Sunday best and was sitting with their families. So Sister Perry left her family alone, went to the back pew, and asked the visitor if she would mind if she sat beside her.

"When the woman smiled in the affirmative, Sister Perry put her arm around her. The next Sunday Sister Perry came to church wearing Levi's and a T-shirt."[10]

---

10. Clayton M. Christensen, *The Power of Everyday Missionaries: The What and How of Sharing the Gospel* (Salt Lake City: Deseret Book, 2013), 139.

Sister Perry didn't just feel annoyed at the sound of the motorcycle disrupting the reverence of the meeting. She didn't just notice the woman walk in and wonder who she was, or just take the good step of inviting the woman to join her family. She *left her family*, went to where this woman sat, and asked to "be with" her.

As important as our families are, if we do not create community for others' children, who will create community for ours? When our kids are the ones in jeans and T-shirts at church, where will their community be? When we are, will there be a community for us? We cannot afford to be so busy building Zion that we ignore our own families. But neither can we afford to be so busy with our own households that we have no time to build Zion.

MY TEACHERS IN COMMUNITY BUILDING

When my daughter felt repeated small impressions to take on the task of building community, she read a lot of books, talked to a lot of people, and felt inspired to try, but she was unsure how to begin. As she prayed for guidance, the answer she felt was, "You know how to do this. Build whimsical moments of connection, like Grandpa Ulrich. Welcome people into your home, like Grandma Great. Act on spiritual promptings, like Grandma Woolsey. Be warm and affectionate, like Granddaddy. Be strong and courageous when it is hard, like Tracy." Each of these little reminders came with a mental image, like Grandpa Ulrich creating a contest to see which of his grandkids could find the biggest cow pie in the pasture (complete with blue ribbons). Or Tracy, her uncle, keeping in touch with his friends while fighting cancer.

I'm betting you too have seen many examples of powerful community builders doing their work. Perhaps my list of such mental images might inspire you too: Write thank-you notes and cheerlead, like Dave. Share what you know generously, like Karen. Use your training to help, like Dr. Chris. Passionately point out others' strengths, like Deanna. Exemplify consistency and courage, like Melanie. Create great ward activities, like Maren D. Serve individuals without complaint, like Michael. Even if you don't feel belonging, create it for others, like John. Build the next generation, like Monika. Treat everyone as if each person were your best friend, like Jan. Show up every day, like Mike. Organize a team, like Kathleen. Celebrate life and lives, like Chris. Joke around, like Kelly. Go to girls' camp, like Carla. Do a ward play, like Nancy. Start a dinner group, like Carrie.

I can't do all of these things, and because others do, I don't need to. But yes, when the student is ready, the teacher will come, and when I start to worry about the rising generation and realize how much we all need community, I am empowered by these powerful teachers with visions of dozens of places to begin. And maybe I can add to that list, "Teach Sunday School in a way that builds community. Like Wendy."

The duties of the teacher's office remind us all, male and female, young and old, that it is our holy responsibility and privilege to build Zion communities and create belonging for ourselves and others as we watch over, strengthen, exhort, invite, warn, teach, and are simply "with" one another in the family of God.

Chapter 6
VISIT EACH HOUSE WITH ORDINANCES
PRIEST

Reading the experience of others, or the revelation given to them, can never give us a comprehensive view of our condition and true relation to God. Knowledge of these things can only be obtained by experience through the ordinances of God set forth for that purpose.

JOSEPH SMITH

The word *priest* generally refers to someone who performs the rites (we would say *ordinances*) of a religion. While we in the restored Church of Jesus Christ conceptualize priesthood broadly as the power and authority to act in God's name in all aspects of Church governance, the office of a priest still specifically entails administering ordinances: baptizing new members and blessing the sacrament we partake of each week in worship services. Priests are also to teach (as are all other priesthood officers) and to visit members in their homes (as are teachers), but one must be at least a priest to perform an ordinance.

While it is not hard to imagine how I, as a woman, might tap into the priesthood power available to a deacon or teacher, it is not immediately clear how that is going to work with the role of a priest. I'm not authorized to baptize people or bless the sacrament,

PRIESTHOOD POWER THROUGH PRIESTHOOD RESPONSIBILITIES

> **DUTIES OF THE OFFICE OF PRIEST**
>
> - "Baptize" (D&C 20:46)
> - "Administer the sacrament" (v. 46)
> - "Visit the house of each member, and exhort them to pray vocally and in secret and attend to all family duties" (v. 47)
> - "Ordain other priests, teachers, and deacons" (v. 48)
> - "Take the lead of meetings when there is no elder present" (v. 49)
> - "Warn, expound, exhort, and teach, and invite all to come unto Christ" (v. 59)

so is the role of a priest something I would ever be involved in?

I am convinced that it is. But just as women could grow in priesthood power by looking at the historical roles of a deacon or teacher, so women might better imagine how to participate in the power of a priest by considering the history of that role.

PRIESTHOOD IN THE TEMPLE

Under the law of Moses, priests descended from Aaron performed temple rites. Only one temple ordinance, baptism for the dead, is performed today by young men holding the office of a priest, but performing ordinances is still what sets a priest apart from deacons or teachers.

Curiously, there is no biblical record of priests as an office in the New Testament Church. Our history of that time period is of course incomplete, so this might simply be an omission, but early Christians would also have associated the word *priest* with Jewish priests of the lineage of Aaron who functioned primarily in the temple. Since Jesus was not of that lineage, nor was the early Christian Church centered in the Jewish temple, destroyed in AD 70, at minimum the word *priest* would have had to take on new meaning to be used in Christianity, and apparently that did not happen right away.

The epistle to the Hebrews makes explicit Jesus Christ's role as the great High Priest of God, however. We also believe He gave priesthood authority to His Apostles, who gave it to others (see John 15:16; Mark 3:14; Acts 14:23). Christ holds the ultimate keys by which priests in His Church in all ages perform the rites and ordinances He requires in the Church and in the temple (Daniel 7:13–14).

Christ fulfilled the purpose of temple sacrifices performed by priests under the law of Moses, replacing them with baptism and partaking of bread and wine in remembrance of the Savior.[1] These ordinances are to be performed with exactness, using only prescribed forms and wording and under priesthood oversight. They express and enact God's covenant with us to be our God and to claim us as His people (see Jeremiah 31:33). However, Isaiah sees that in the last days, "The earth also is defiled under the inhabitants thereof; because they have transgressed the laws, *changed the ordinance, broken the everlasting covenant*" (Isaiah 24:5; emphasis added).

Without the voice of the Lord through His servants the prophets, people will stray from the meaning ordinances are intended to convey, interpreting or reinventing them in their own way: "The day cometh that they who will not hear the voice of the Lord, neither the voice of his servants, neither give heed to the words of the prophets and apostles, shall be cut off from among the people; For they have *strayed from mine ordinances,* and have *broken mine everlasting covenant;* They seek not the Lord to establish his righteousness, but every man walketh in his own way, and after the image of his own god" (D&C 1:14–16; emphasis added).

With similar attention to exactness and under the oversight of those who hold priesthood keys, both women and men officiate in priesthood ordinances in the temples today. President M. Russell Ballard has said, "The endowment is literally a gift of power. All who enter the house of the Lord officiate in the ordinances of

---

[1]. Other sacred ordinances not spoken of publicly are also referenced in records from the New Testament period.

the priesthood."[2] Think about that second sentence in particular. Ordinance workers are set apart with priesthood authority to officiate in temple ordinances for the living. But they are not "all who enter the house of the Lord." It sounds like patrons also officiate in vicarious ordinances for the dead, performing this priestly role during their own temple experience.

I will use the word *priestly* repeatedly in this chapter. When I use the word *motherly*, it can mean a couple of things: 1) a person is acting in a way characteristic of mothers even though he or she is not a mother, as in, "Dad was especially motherly toward me when I got hurt"; or 2) someone is actually a mother and acting like one, as in, "I noticed her intense motherly love for her adopted son." When we speak of someone acting in a *priestly role*, then, it could imply acting in a way characteristic of priests even without being one, or it could imply actually being a priest and performing functions related to that priesthood. I won't try to parse which definition applies when but will leave it to your own reflection.

Consistent with the rich tradition of the role of priests in temple worship, I see evidence that in the temple women and men alike

- are vested and consecrated as "a kingdom of priests" to officiate in priesthood ordinances (Exodus 19:6);
- are endowed with priesthood authority and power to create and bless covenant families in time and eternity within God's "house of order" (D&C 132:18);
- participate in the "ministering of angels" promised through the Aaronic Priesthood, particularly as they participate in family history and in temple work for the dead (D&C 107:20).

Let's look at some of that evidence.

---

2. "Men and Women and Priesthood Power," *Ensign*, September 2014.

A KINGDOM OF PRIESTS

One of my favorite places to visit in Jerusalem is the Holy Temple Visitors' Center run by the Temple Institute. No, they don't have missionaries with black name tags welcoming visitors at this temple visitors' center. The temple visitors are being introduced to here is Solomon's Temple and its anticipated reconstruction. This visitors' center is a kind of living museum that displays painstakingly recreated furnishings, musical instruments, altars, clothing, and other sacred objects the priests would have used and worn as they carried out their work in the temple. The purpose of the institute is not just to memorialize the past, however, but to prepare for the future day when, as the Temple Institute founders hope and believe, a Jewish temple will again be built on Mount Moriah. Right now what stands on Mount Moriah is one of the holiest shrines of Islam, so I get pretty nervous about the large mural in the Temple Institute that depicts modern-day Jews excitedly building a Jewish temple on that exact spot (a picture complete with cranes and a monorail). But I am fascinated by the carefully recreated structure that disperses water for an order of priests to ritually wash with before entering the temple. I especially love an artist's rendering of priests helping one another dress in long white robes, round white turbans, and colored sashes to begin their temple service. We see other priests dispersing neatly folded packets of this temple clothing from stacks on open shelves. It is an oddly familiar sight.

It is also a simple reminder that all those who washed and then dressed in this sacred clothing as they entered the holy temple were priests.

Anciently, the direct descendants of Aaron were the only legitimate heirs to the priesthood; however, before they actually became priests they had to be consecrated to, or vested with, their priestly office upon reaching adulthood (see Exodus 28:41). This was done through special ceremonies and sacrifices described in the Bible

PRIESTHOOD POWER THROUGH PRIESTHOOD RESPONSIBILITIES

Dictionary as follows: "(1) They were washed at the door of the tabernacle. (2) They were clothed with the priestly garments (coats, girdles, and . . . turbans). (3) They were anointed . . . with holy oil. [They offered] . . . three sacrifices: (1) . . . a sin offering, to put away their sin; (2) . . . a burnt offering, to indicate the full and complete surrender of themselves to God; (3) . . . a peace or consecration offering. . . . The priest's hands were filled . . . with [parts of the sacrificial] offering. The gifts that henceforward they would offer to the Lord on behalf of the people were thus committed to them."

In similar fashion, women and men who attend the temple today are initiated into and endowed or vested with priestly identities.

Today in our temples, women along with men perform temple ordinances with priesthood authority. Both women and men are set apart as "temple *ordinance* workers" for this straightforward purpose. Women and men temple patrons are also prepared by their service to officiate thereafter in providing temple ordinances for others. Both women and men, prepared by their own endowment, can be set apart as temple workers and given priesthood authority by temple presidencies to officiate in priesthood ordinances that are essential to salvation and officially recorded.

President Dallin H. Oaks verifies: "With the exception of the sacred work that sisters do in the temple under the keys held by the temple president, which I will describe hereafter, only one who holds a priesthood office can officiate in a priesthood ordinance. And all authorized priesthood ordinances are recorded on the records of the Church."[3]

President Joseph Fielding Smith, then President of the Quorum of the Twelve Apostles, said in a talk to the sisters (parts of which were quoted by President Dallin H. Oaks in the April 2014 general conference): "A [sister] may have authority given

---

3. Dallin H. Oaks, "The Keys and Authority of the Priesthood," *Ensign*, May 2014.

to . . . her, to do certain things in the Church that are binding and absolutely necessary for our salvation, such as the work that our sisters do in the House of the Lord. . . . you sisters who labor in the House of the Lord can lay your hands upon your sisters . . . with divine authority, because the Lord recognizes positions, which you occupy. . . . It is within the privilege of the sisters of this Church to . . . receive authority and power as queens and priestesses."[4]

On the Church's official website, the Gospel Topics section includes essays that seminary and institute teachers have reportedly been instructed to learn like the back of their hands. In the article "Joseph Smith's Teachings about Priesthood, Temple, and Women," we read: "Joseph Smith spoke of establishing among the Relief Society sisters a 'kingdom of priests.' He had used similar terms earlier when speaking of the relationship of all the Saints to the temple. This 'kingdom of priests' would be comprised of men and women who made temple covenants.

". . . The priesthood authority exercised by Latter-day Saint women in the temple and elsewhere remains largely unrecognized by people outside the Church and is sometimes misunderstood or overlooked by those within. Latter-day Saints and others often mistakenly equate priesthood with religious office and the men who hold it, which obscures the broader Latter-day Saint concept of priesthood."

We notice repeated priesthood references used in the temple in initiating and instructing both women and men to prepare them to officiate in temple ordinances, minister in the work of angels, and enter God's presence.

Some of the roles or privileges associated with the priesthood in ancient and modern times include

---

4. "Relief Society—An Aid to the Priesthood," address delivered at the Officers Meeting, Relief Society General Conference, October 8, 1958. Printed in the *Relief Society Magazine*, 46:4, (January 1959).

- pronouncing blessings (see Deuteronomy 21:5; D&C 107:53);
- officially assuring forgiveness of sin (see Leviticus 5:10; Bible Dictionary, "Confession");
- anointing others into priestly roles (see Exodus 40:12–15);
- sealing and confirming blessings (see Guide to the Scriptures, "Anoint"; D&C 42:44);
- using the laying on of hands to offer blessings of health, confer priestly office, or convey the Spirit (see Numbers 27:23; 2 Timothy 1:6; James 5:14–15; Alma 6:1; D&C 33:15; 107:65–67);
- promising an outpouring of the Spirit upon others (see Acts 9:17; 1 Nephi 13:37);
- overseeing the correct administration of priesthood ordinances (see Moroni 4:1; 3 Nephi 18:5–6);
- representing heavenly messengers in bringing people into the presence of God (see D&C 84:14–23; Joseph Smith Translation, Exodus 34:1–2; Jacob 1:7–8).

I find it interesting to contemplate this list side by side with what I see both female and male ordinance workers do in the temple.

Going back to the role of a priest today, I note that the priest offering the sacrament prayer recites, "*We* ask thee in the name of thy Son, Jesus Christ, to bless and sanctify this bread to the souls of all those who partake of it" (D&C 20:77; emphasis added). I am not really clear if this "we" includes only the priests at the table or the priesthood holders standing ready to distribute the sacrament to the congregation, or if the priest's "we" represents every person, male or female, whose head is bowed in worship and who says "amen" to that prayer. The preceding verse prescribes that "*he* shall kneel with the church" and does not prescribe that more than one priest must be present, suggesting the possibility that "we" includes all in the meeting who join this prayer. In other words, I think it is possible that one small way I can participate in the blessing prayer of a priest is to join his petitioning of the Lord on behalf of the congregation.

That's a sweet possibility that brings meaning and power to the sacrament prayers to me, but I'm not absolutely sure it is what God intended by that word, "we." But when, as a temple worker, I spoke the words of a temple ordinance in the name of Jesus Christ and with His authority, there was no ambiguity. I was authorized as surely as were the sons of Aaron to bless my sisters in God's house. If I so qualified, I knew the power of God could also attend those ministrations (see Moroni 3:4; D&C 18:32).

To summarize, like priests of old, in the temple women and men 1) study the law and plan of God, 2) enter covenants with Him, and 3) are vested (meaning clothed, given rights, or gifted with power) and consecrated (meaning set apart to a holy purpose) in priestly roles so we can officiate in the temple on behalf of others. Every time we return to the temple, we do so to act in the sacred office of extending these same rights and blessings to others.

Clearly women are welcome, needed, even crucial to the priesthood work of saving the family of God as a "kingdom of priests."

PUTTING GOD'S HOUSE IN ORDER

As outlined in the Doctrine and Covenants, the work of priests includes visiting the house of each family and exhorting them to prayer and family duty (see D&C 20:47). I believe researching family history work is one way women and men can, with priesthood power, *visit the house of each family*—each family in their own family lineage and ultimately each family in the entire world—to see that each house is in order with its relationships properly recorded (see D&C 128:1–9), and to offer each family the privilege of receiving necessary ordinances and covenants of the temple. Not everyone holds the office of a priest, but perhaps those who do genealogical research, record family histories, and perform temple work for the dead are in one sense participating in crucial duties of that office. They visit the houses of their extended family and help order them within the covenants of the priesthood.

All the youth of the Church today can operate either in the offices, or after the patterns, of the Aaronic Priesthood. They have been promised particular blessings for participating in this sacred work: "I invite the young people of the Church to learn about and experience the Spirit of Elijah. I encourage you to study, to search out your ancestors, and to prepare yourselves to perform proxy baptisms in the house of the Lord for your kindred dead (see D&C 124:28–36). And I urge you to help other people identify their family histories.

"As you respond in faith to this invitation, your hearts shall turn to the fathers. The promises made to Abraham, Isaac, and Jacob will be implanted in your hearts. Your patriarchal blessing, with its declaration of lineage, will link you to these fathers and be more meaningful to you. Your love and gratitude for your ancestors will increase. Your testimony of and conversion to the Savior will become deep and abiding. And I promise you will be protected against the intensifying influence of the adversary. As you participate in and love this holy work, you will be safeguarded in your youth and throughout your lives."[5]

Youth and adults alike find that using the computer to find their ancestors brings a sense of satisfaction and joy that playing a video game can't replicate. Searching family names teaches us practical skills of patience, work, and attention to detail. It may help us "study and learn, and become acquainted with all good books,

---

5. David A. Bednar, "The Hearts of the Children Shall Turn," *Ensign*, November 2012. See also https://www.lds.org/topics/family-history/fdd-cook/blessings-video?lang=eng&old=true.

and with languages, tongues, and people" (D&C 90:15) as well as "obtain a knowledge of history, and of countries, and of kingdoms, of laws of God and man, and all this for the salvation of Zion" (D&C 93:53).

I confess that searching out names and doing temple work for the dead doesn't completely make sense to me in a rational way. But this much I do know: something outside of myself helps me find the names of these people. I know from strong spiritual impressions and experiences that at least some of them very much want this work done.

As one example, I remember many years ago when personal computers were still a pipe dream and my husband and I were leaving BYU to move to California for school. The last fast Sunday before our move, I headed up to the university library genealogy facilities to take advantage of this library one last time before heading to our new and soon-to-be even busier life as graduate students. When I got to the library, however, I realized I hadn't thought this through very well. I wasn't sure where to begin or what needed to be done. I prayed for help, and I felt that I should look for the then-required record of my grandparents' marriage so I could have them sealed.

This seemed a little odd to me. My grandmother's great-grandparents had joined the Church in Kirtland in 1830, crossed the plains, and settled in Springville. She had lived in Utah all her life, even though she had never been active and seemed to know almost nothing about the Church. My grandfather was not a member at all, despite also living in Salt Lake City for decades. Surely they had had ample opportunity to choose the gospel and qualify for this ordinance if they had wanted. But I blithely went off to the library to find their marriage certificate.

On my arrival, I found four or five large reels of microfilm for marriage records for Utah for the time period in question. There was no index or search engine—I just went through all of them as quickly as I could. I was almost done and had found nothing when I heard the announcement: "The library will close in fifteen minutes." I was sure I must have missed their record by skimming too quickly, but I was out of time to go through them all again. I prayed for help and randomly chose one film to review a second time, loaded it onto the film reader, and started again to crank the handle that turned the reel of blurry copies of old marriage records. The announcement came, "The library will close in five minutes." I paused to send the thought heavenward, "Okay, Grandmother, if you really want this done I need your help. Now." I turned the crank again. Nothing. I turned it again. And there on the page before me was the familiar handwriting and signature of my grandmother on her marriage license.

I could hardly believe it. It was as if I had recognized her handwriting even before I recognized her name. With a minute to spare, I made the then-required copy to submit to the temple department to clear the way for this ordinance to be done. As soon as I got home I called my mother, the family genealogist, to tell her excitedly of my experience. She was quiet, which confused me, as my mother was always up for a great miracle story. Then she said, "That's really sweet, Wendy, but I did all the temple work for your grandparents years ago. This has already all been taken care of." Huh. Well, that kind of popped my miracle bubble. Now I was the one who was quiet. Oh well.

But the next day my mother called me back. "This is very interesting," she said. "I looked up my records of your grandparents, and I was right. Their baptisms and endowments have all been done, just as I thought. But they were never sealed to each other. I don't know why. And I don't know how long it would have taken me to discover this, since I was so sure their temple work was all completed." My mother didn't know my grandparents had not been sealed. I didn't know it. But apparently my grandmother knew it. My first visit with my husband to the Los Angeles Temple after our move was to do this work for my grandparents—work I know they wanted done, work my mother thought had been done, work I thought they had had ample opportunity to do for themselves if it had mattered to them.

This and other experiences convince me that family history matters. Temple sealings matter. I don't recognize the signatures of the other ancestors whose records or names I've sought out, but I do recognize the signature of God in the joy I feel doing this work and in the many "coincidences" that have brought their names out of obscurity and into my hands. Priesthood power is evident in many ways when I am engaged in this work. I have personally experienced that power as I have been able to understand foreign languages, locate obscure relatives in small foreign towns, read illegible documents, see glimpses of the spirit world, and even find parents my immediate family members did not know they had.

Learning family stories can be as important as learning family names in strengthening youth and adults alike to live with resilience and courage. A research study in progress in New York City when the World Trade Centers were attacked on 9/11 in 2001 had been looking at how much children knew about the stories of their parents' and grandparents' lives. After the attack, the researchers went back to these children to see how they were faring. The children who knew the most about their family stories were coping significantly better than those who did not.

One of the researchers shares his conclusion: "Among our most powerful findings was that the more children knew about the history of their families *(both the good and the bad things in their history!)* the stronger they were, the more resilient, the higher their self-esteem, the better their families functioned, the less likely they were to have difficulties in adjustment. Knowledge of family history, it turned out, was crucially important to well-being. Through the stories that they hear at dinner tables, on vacations, on holidays, etc., children learn about their family histories. Thus, our broad conclusion was and still is that family stories are health-giving and immunizing."[6]

A woman I'll call Jessica had postponed filing for divorce for several years, hoping that things would work out with her husband. They pursued counseling at length, and she fasted, prayed, studied her patriarchal blessing, and acted on any spiritual impression that came to her in her efforts to improve herself, change her marriage, and know the Lord's will. She had never even imagined the possibility of divorce, and was sure that if she just tried hard enough her marriage would succeed. But things got worse instead of better. One night she was looking at a picture of Jesus Christ on the wall of her home as she prayed for guidance. Her husband had moved out over a year before and would not tell her where he lived. He was dating other people, said he didn't love her, and was unwilling to recommit to their marriage. Yet she also knew she would have to be the one to file for divorce. As she prayed that night, she remembered being told stories about her great-grandmother, Martha, widowed while pregnant with her fourth child after just six years of marriage. Years later Martha had remarried, but after a decade of struggle she "gave back the ring" to this second husband, as the family story went. Jessica suddenly realized she was not the first person in her ancestry to face such a painful decision. As she looked at the picture of Jesus Christ and contemplated "giving the ring back" to her husband, she felt as if the Savior were holding

---

6. Marshal P. Duke, "*A Voyage Homeward:* Fiction and Family Stories—Resilience and Rehabilitation," *The Journal of Humanities in Rehabilitation* website, posted July 8, 2015, https://scholarblogs.emory.edu/journalofhumanitiesinrehabilitation/2015/07/08/a-voyage-homeward-fiction-and-family-storiesresilience-and-rehabilitation. See also Duke M, Fivush R, Lazarus A. (2008), "Knowledge of family history as a clinically useful index of psychological well-being and prognosis," *Psychotherapy,* 45:268–72.

out His hand to her, saying, "Give the ring to me. Your covenant is with me, and you have fulfilled that covenant. It is time to move forward. This decision is not just between you and your husband, but between you and me. You have done all you can. Give the ring to me." The story of her faithful great-grandmother, whom she had never met, helped Jessica connect with the guidance of the Spirit. It gave her courage to lose her marriage without losing her hope or herself.

THE MINISTERING OF ANGELS

A biography of the life of General George S. Patton, known as one of the most successful combat generals in US history, describes a time when Patton, as a young lieutenant colonel, was under heavy fire in France during World War I. Patton looked up and saw in the clouds above him *images of his ancestors*, some of whom had fought in the Civil War before Patton was born. Patton somehow understood what he needed to do: charge the enemy. He did so with a few others, was wounded, and lay on the field of battle hoping for evacuation when he felt "overwhelmed by a deep feeling of warmth and peace and comfort, and of love. I knew profoundly death was related to life; how unimportant the change-over was; how ever-lasting the soul—and the love was all around me, like a subdued light."[7]

As this story demonstrates, people with and without the Aaronic Priesthood may receive the ministering of angels, just as people with or without the gift of the Holy Ghost may feel His influence. But the Aaronic Priesthood holds the keys of the ministering of angels (see D&C 107:20), and Joseph Smith declared to the sisters of the Relief Society, which was organized under the authority of the priesthood and after the pattern of the priesthood,

---

7. In Carlos d'Este, *A Genius for War: A Life of General George S. Patton* (London: Harper Collins, 1995), 260–61.

"If you live up to your privileges, angels cannot be restrained from being your associates."[8]

And who are the angels that are most likely to minister to us? During the siege of a Wyoming elementary school in a community predominantly made up of members of The Church of Jesus Christ of Latter-day Saints, a deranged man and his wife held 154 students and teachers hostage for $300,000,000 ransom in a room containing a large homemade bomb. Eventually the bomb was detonated by accident, but all of the hostages were able to escape, although half of them were seriously burned or injured. Several of the children later reported seeing and hearing instructions from angels in the room—women, whom the children did not recognize but from whom they felt great love and comfort. Later several of these boys and girls independently identified the angels they had seen from pictures in family albums as deceased grandmothers and an aunt.[9]

President Joseph F. Smith once taught: "I believe we move and have our being in the presence of heavenly messengers and of heavenly beings. We are not separate from them. . . . We are closely related to our kindred, to our ancestors . . . who have preceded us into the spirit world. We cannot forget them; we do not cease to love them; we always hold them in our hearts, in memory, and thus we are associated and united to them by ties that we cannot break. . . . If this is the case with us in our finite condition, surrounded by our mortal weaknesses, . . . how much more certain it is . . . to believe that those who have been faithful, who have gone beyond . . . can see us better than we can see them; that they know us better than we know them. . . . We live in their presence, they see us, they are solicitous for our welfare, they love us now more than ever. For now they see the dangers that beset us; . . . their love

---

8. Joseph Smith, in Relief Society Minute Book, Nauvoo, Illinois, April 28, 1842, 39.
9. See http://www.ldsliving.com/the-Cokeville-miracle/s/79933.

for us and their desire for our wellbeing must be greater than that which we feel for ourselves."[10]

I wonder if the work we do for the dead in temples helps clear the way for them to minister to us and our loved ones. Is this part of the urgency we feel to provide these ordinances for those who "are solicitous for our welfare, . . . see the dangers that beset us . . . [and] desire . . . our wellbeing"? With access to priesthood power and the blessings of the endowment, are they more able to act on behalf of their posterity and extended family, and ours?

Elder Jeffrey R. Holland taught that the work of angels is carried out by both immortal and mortal beings. He says of angels: "Usually such beings are *not* seen. Sometimes they are. But seen or unseen they are *always* near. Sometimes their assignments are very grand and have significance for the whole world. Sometimes the messages are more private. Occasionally the angelic purpose is to warn. But most often it is to comfort, to provide some form of merciful attention, guidance in difficult times.

". . . . Not all angels are from the other side of the veil. Some of them we walk with and talk with—here, now, every day. Some of them reside in our own neighborhoods. Some of them gave birth to us, and in my case, one of them consented to marry me. Indeed heaven never seems closer than when we see the love of God manifested in the kindness and devotion of people so good and so pure that *angelic* is the only word that comes to mind."[11]

Elder Holland recounts the story of a seven-year-old boy on the far side of a raging river, praying for help, who sees a being in white coming toward him. He wonders if it is an angel sent to his rescue. And it is. His father, worried for his son's safety and realizing he must be on the other side of the river, has stripped

---

10. In Conference Report, April 1916, 2–3; see also *Gospel Doctrine,* 5th ed. (1939), 430–31.
11. Jeffrey R. Holland, "The Ministry of Angels," *Ensign,* November 2008.

down to his long thermal underwear and swum across to find him. Elder Holland concludes: "On occasions, global or personal, we may feel we are distanced from God, shut out from heaven, lost, alone in dark and dreary places. Often enough that distress can be of our own making, but even then the Father of us all is watching and assisting. And always there are those angels who come and go all around us, seen and unseen, known and unknown, mortal and immortal."[12]

With the very power that angels from beyond the veil access to protect, warn, and bless us here, women and men today may not only receive the ministering of angels but participate in their work among God's children on both sides of the veil. Nephi assures us that those who receive the gift of the Holy Ghost "could speak with the tongue of angels" (2 Nephi 32:2). What does this mean? Apparently it means to speak and teach the words of Christ from the scriptures by the power of the Holy Ghost: "Angels speak by the power of the Holy Ghost; wherefore, they speak the words of Christ. Wherefore, I said unto you, feast upon the words of Christ; for behold, the words of Christ will tell you all things what ye should do. Wherefore, now after I have spoken these words, if ye cannot understand them it will be because ye ask not, neither do ye knock; wherefore, ye are not brought into the light, but must perish in the dark" (2 Nephi 32:3–4).

How can we as women and men today participate in the privilege of receiving the ministering of angels? In my experience, the likelihood of such experiences increases substantially when I am engaged in family history research, doing temple work for the dead as a worker or patron, recording and sharing family stories with my loved ones, doing all I can to seek and follow the promptings of the

---

12. Holland, "The Ministry of Angels."

Holy Ghost as I try to build Zion, and empowering others with the words of Christ.

And how can I myself do the work of angels, becoming a messenger of salvation to others? Same answer.

Historically, the ordinances conducted by priests in the temple pointed God's covenant people to the great and eternal sacrifice of Jesus Christ. That has not changed. Yet the majority of those ancient people and their priests failed to connect those ordinances with conversion to Jesus Christ. Though ordinances pointed them toward Him, He never became their personal Messiah, Redeemer, and High Priest of good things to come. We also risk performing temple ordinances in a ritualistic way that is exact and true to form but that does not connect us with angels or with our Father and Savior.

Indeed, the temple is not the story of the life of Jesus Christ in any obvious sense. But it is the story of how He redeems us and how we can find our way back to Him and our Heavenly Parents. It shows us how fallen people can repent and change, take upon themselves the name of Christ, and be empowered by His gospel. It endows ordinary mortals with priestly roles and with priestly power to become true messengers of salvation to others, bringing them to the gate of heaven. And it teaches us to empower both our ancestors and our posterity to do the same. We gain priesthood power as we participate in temple ordinances with prayerful hearts, alert minds, honest study, a sincere desire to know God's will, and confidence in our privileges.

Chapter 7

HEAL AND CONFIRM WITH THE HOLY GHOST

ELDER

The power to speak and act in God's name requires revelation and ... to have it when we need it requires praying and working in faith for the companionship of the Holy Ghost.

—Henry B. Eyring

President M. Russell Ballard has counseled the women of the Church, "Like faithful sisters in the past, you need to learn how to use the priesthood authority with which you have been endowed to obtain every eternal blessing that will be yours."[1] As mature, *elder* women in the gospel, we want to better understand the nature and source of that authority. We hope to gain "access to the power and the blessings of the priesthood [that] is available to all of God's children,"[2] as encouraged by President Russell M. Nelson. We certainly don't want to encroach on the prerogatives of Melchizedek Priesthood elders, but we also want to fully exercise our own spiritual gifts and impressions within our priesthood-authorized

---

1. "Women of Dedication, Faith, Determination, and Action," BYU Women's Conference address, May 1, 2015.
2. M. Russell Ballard, "Men and Women in the Work of the Lord," *New Era*, April 2014, 4.

assignments, family duties, and covenant responsibilities. We want to be filled with the Holy Ghost as not only our personal companion but as our companion in the work of building Zion, saving souls, and blessing the family of God through priesthood power.

The principles and blessings of priesthood power, we note, are especially associated with the Melchizedek Priesthood, under which men and women acting by office or assignment are given more flexibility, responsibility, leadership roles, and span of influence than associated with the Aaronic Priesthood alone. We learn that those "ordained after the order of Melchizedek" anciently "were righteous and holy men," and that decisions made by Melchizedek Priesthood leaders today "are to be made in all righteousness, in holiness, and lowliness of heart, meekness and long-suffering, and in faith, and virtue, and knowledge, temperance, patience, godliness, brotherly kindness and charity." These virtues are especially important to all who seek the blessings associated with the Melchizedek Priesthood "because the promise is, if these things [listed here] abound in them they shall not be unfruitful in the knowledge of

> **DUTIES OF THE OFFICE OF ELDER**
>
> - "Confirm those who are baptized into the church, by the laying on of hands for the baptism of fire and the Holy Ghost" (D&C 20:41)
> - "Confirm the church by the laying on of the hands, and the giving of the Holy Ghost" (v. 43)
> - Ordain others "by the power of the Holy Ghost" (vv. 39, 60)
> - "Take the lead of all meetings . . . [and] conduct the meetings as they are led by the Holy Ghost, according to the commandments and revelations of God" (vv. 44–45)
> - "Preach the everlasting gospel among the nations" (D&C 36:5)
> - "Lay their hands upon [children of Church members] in the name of Jesus Christ, and bless them in his name" (D&C 20:70)
> - "Pray over [the sick], anointing [them] with oil in the name of the Lord" (James 5:14)

the Lord" (D&C 107:29–31). The kind of "knowledge" referred to here is a personal and intimate knowledge of the Lord (see Ether 3:20; John 17:3; D&C 94:98).

A modern Apostle further counsels that pride and lack of self-restraint interferes with spiritual power: "Humility is a fertile soil where spirituality grows and produces the fruit of inspiration to know what to do. It gives access to divine power. . . . An individual motivated by a desire for praise or recognition will not qualify to be taught by the Spirit. An individual who is arrogant or who lets his or her emotions influence decisions will not be powerfully led by the Spirit. . . . Our obedience assures that when required, we can qualify for divine power to accomplish an inspired objective."[3]

THE DUTIES OF AN ELDER

With that background, let's review the priesthood duties and responsibilities of elders, listed above. Beyond roles shared with the Aaronic Priesthood, elders in the Melchizedek Priesthood are to confirm the newly baptized, confirm the Church, ordain others, take the lead in meetings, preach the gospel to the world, bless children, and anoint and pray for the sick. Let's consider how women can help powerfully create the "mighty realities" for which these Melchizedek Priesthood ordinances and duties stand.[4]

1. Confirm the newly baptized with the gift of the Holy Ghost. Elders have a duty to confirm the newly baptized as members of the Church and authorize them to receive the gift of the Holy Ghost (see Acts 8:15–17). What might be needed, beyond the symbol-laden ordinance, to create the reality of truly becoming

---

3. Richard G. Scott, "How to Obtain Revelation and Inspiration for Your Personal Life," *Ensign*, May 2012.
4. John A. Widtsoe, *Power from on high: Fourth year junior genealogical classes* (Salt Lake City: Genealogical Society of Utah, 1937).

"confirmed" as members of a new community and to actually receive this gift? How is this "mighty reality" created?

An ordinance is like a picture of a promise—a physical act that symbolizes a spiritual reality we can seek.[5] When I think of the *picture* of an elder bestowing the gift of the Holy Ghost, I imagine a spiritual conduit created by the priesthood holder between heaven and earth, a conduit the recipient is helped to visualize, experience, and replicate. I also note that this ordinance generally includes several elders surrounding the person being confirmed. The *picture* created is of a circle of support and love that is both welcoming and protective. It reminds me of the angels who surrounded the children in the New World during the Savior's visit (see 3 Nephi 17:24).

Both men and women can help new members feel and act on the Holy Ghost and can surround them with the love and support this ordinance symbolizes. Ministering brothers and sisters have a particular responsibility and stewardship, ultimately authorized by a bishop with priesthood keys, to empower new members to feel received and confirmed. The spiritual power we are also entitled to can help us see those we minister to as God sees them, listen with greater empathy than comes naturally to us, and respond to spoken and unspoken needs with more creativity and love than we are capable of on our own. We're not trying to simply receive such gifts and power ourselves, however; we're trying to empower these new members to recognize and act on the gifts of the Holy Ghost for themselves, receiving not just us but Him.

2. Confirm the Church with the Holy Ghost. Just two verses after specifying that elders are to confirm "those who are baptized into the church" and bestow the gift of the Holy Ghost, the Lord specifies that elders are also to "confirm the church by the laying on of the hands, and the giving of the Holy Ghost" (D&C 20:41, 43).

---

5. See Kathleen Flake, "Supping with the Lord: A liturgical theology of the LDS sacrament," *Sunstone* (1993), 18–27.

It sounds as though these might refer to two different groups, the second being those already in the Church who still need to know they belong and need to receive the Holy Ghost in an ongoing way.

President Gordon B. Hinckley taught the missionaries that every new convert needs a friend, a responsibility, and to be nourished by the good word of God.[6] So do missionaries returning from full-time service, new people moving into a ward, young adults both single and married, children coming into the youth program, anyone facing a time of transition or change—in short, every member of the Church needs mentoring and confirmation from others in order to be mentored and confirmed by the Lord. Both women and men can be empowered by the Holy Ghost to do this welcoming, mentoring, "confirming" work for the Church at large.

The idea of ongoing growth and confirmation with the Holy Ghost is supported by Joseph Smith's dedicatory prayer of the Kirtland Temple: "And do thou grant, Holy Father, that all those who shall worship in this house may . . . grow up in thee, and *receive a fulness of the Holy Ghost,* and be organized according to thy laws, and be prepared to obtain every needful thing" (D&C 109:14–15; emphasis added).

Elder Richard G. Scott reminds us that this spiritual power is learned through experience and struggle and that it will become easier as we "consistently strive to recognize and follow feelings prompted by the Spirit. . . . I witness that as you gain experience and success in being guided by the Spirit, your confidence in the impressions you feel can become more certain than your dependence on what you see or hear."[7] Elder Scott goes on to say, "Spirituality yields two fruits. The first is inspiration to know what

---

6. See Gordon B. Hinckley, "Find the Lambs, Feed the Sheep," *Ensign,* May 1999.
7. Richard G. Scott, "To Acquire Spiritual Guidance," *Ensign,* November 2009.

to do. The second is power, or the capacity to do it."[8] Women with priesthood authority have the right to the inspiration to know what to do as well as the power to do it. Female and male temple workers also help "confirm the Church" with a fullness of the Spirit through temple ordinances.

3. Ordain others according to the gifts of the Holy Ghost. It is the duty of an elder "to ordain other elders, priests, teachers, and deacons . . . according to the gifts and callings of God unto him; and he is to be ordained by the power of the Holy Ghost, which is in the one who ordains him" (D&C 20:39, 60). Again we see the importance of the power of the Holy Ghost in this act of conferring priesthood authority and power to others. The ordinance is valid even if the one performing it lacks the power of the Holy Ghost, but it is the *duty* of an elder to obtain and use such power.

When the revelation describing the duties of priesthood offices was given, the word *ordain* was also used for women. Emma Smith was to be "ordained" by Joseph Smith to expound scriptures and exhort the Church (D&C 25:7), even though today we would say she was to be "set apart" or "blessed." Clearly those setting women apart to callings have as much duty to do so by the power of the Holy Ghost as those ordaining men, and women thus set apart have as much right to the Spirit in fulfilling their duties as those ordained have.

4. Take the lead of meetings as led by the Holy Ghost. Elders are "to take the lead of all meetings" and "conduct the meetings as they are led by the Holy Ghost, according to the commandments and revelations of God" (D&C 20:44–45). When authorized, women also take the lead of many meetings in the Church, and may conduct the women's session of general conference; ward and stake Relief Society, Young Women, and Primary meetings; various

---

8. Scott, "To Acquire Spiritual Guidance."

committee, training, and presidency meetings; and family councils. The one conducting is to be led by the Holy Ghost.

I was once asked by the Young Women General President to make a brief presentation to a Church committee that included both male and female General Officers of the Church and several Church employees. She stood to conduct the meeting, called on a member of the Young Men General Presidency to pray, and introduced me. In the absence of a presiding General Authority, her leadership role was equal in this setting to that of the Young Men General President who served with her. I was reminded that a man does not automatically have authority to preside, conduct, or make decisions by virtue of his priesthood office alone, but only by virtue of his specific calling and keys. Thus a Young Men president, a Young Women president, a Primary president, and a Sunday School president in a ward or stake serve as equals under the presiding authority of the bishop or stake president.

As another example, I served as both a Relief Society president and a stake Relief Society president under Bishop Nielson, who was first my bishop and then my stake president. In both settings, he asked me to convene and lead a periodic meeting with the Young Women and Primary presidents to talk about the staffing needs of our organizations. He asked that we prayerfully make decisions together about who we felt could be called to various positions in these auxiliaries. Each president met first with her counselors to discuss these matters, and then we counseled together as presidents before making our united recommendations to Bishop Nielson. He specifically asked me as Relief Society president to make sure that the needs of the Young Women and Primary came first, as well as the needs of the individual women being asked to serve. The needs of the Relief Society as an organization came last. Under this clear mandate, none of us rushed to be the first to snatch up a capable move-in, hoarded our favorite teacher, or complained that our inspiration was being ignored in favor of someone else's. Bishop Nielson, privy to information we did not have and holding the keys of presidency, sometimes had different insight about who should be called where, but we all felt respected and heard by one another and by him. I remember feeling keenly the responsibility that I had been given to "take the lead" in this meeting in a way that would serve and strengthen everyone.

5. Take the gospel to others. President Dallin H. Oaks has specifically stated, "When a woman—young or old—is set apart to preach the gospel as a full-time missionary, she is given priesthood authority to perform a priesthood function."[9] My grandmother was the first, and for a while the only, sister missionary in her mission in the early 1900s. She was the first of four generations of sister missionaries in my family—to date. The Church authorizes its youngest adults to carry on the crucial work of taking the gospel to the nations, an example to me of our institutional commitment to humility and faith as the instruments of spiritual power: "And if men come unto me I will show unto them their weakness. I give unto men weakness that they may be humble; and my grace is sufficient for all men that humble themselves before me; for if they humble themselves before me, and have faith in me, then will I make weak things become strong unto them" (Ether 12:27).

Sister missionaries are of course not the only women who can participate in the priesthood duty of taking the gospel to others. Whether or not they are *authorized* as full-time missionaries, women and men, youth and children, are all invited to participate in this sacred work. As just one example, our daughter serving a mission in Taiwan once wrote to ask us who we thought was the most important person in a ward to the success of missionary work. Her conclusion? Primary teachers. When she brought an

---

9. Dallin H. Oaks, "The Keys and Authority of the Priesthood," *Ensign*, May 2014.

investigating family to church, if the children enjoyed Primary, the parents and children returned. If Primary wasn't a hit, they usually did not. The Primary teachers, male or female, were not formally authorized as official representatives of the Church as my daughter was, but both missionaries and Primary teachers can participate with power in the priesthood duty of taking the gospel to others.

6. Bless children in the name of Christ. In addition to the duties of priesthood offices, Doctrine and Covenants 20 describes the duties of Church members. We read, "Every member of the church of Christ having children is to bring them unto the elders before the church, who are to lay their hands upon them in the name of Jesus Christ, and bless them in his name" (D&C 20:70).

The symbolism of blessing children by the laying on of hands draws on our very first experiences with mothers and fathers who touch us with wonder and love. Physical touch is crucial to the physical, emotional, and intellectual development of infants and children. In one study, premature infants who were gently massaged for just fifteen minutes a day gained weight forty-seven percent more quickly and could be released from the hospital days earlier than those who were not held and touched, even though the first group did not actually eat more. Infants who have been touched more make gains in motor and intellectual development that are sustained months and even years later. Children who have been traumatized recover better and faster when lovingly and safely held and soothed. Touch not only communicates affection and connection but helps *confirm* in children a sense of belonging and family identity. Chemicals released in the brain in the presence of touch, or in its absence, seem to account for these differences.[10]

Giving children blessings communicates affection from the

---

10. See Daniel Goleman (1988), "The experience of touch: research points to a critical role," *New York Times Archives,* https://www.nytimes.com/1988/02/02/science/the-experience-of-touch-research-points-to-a-critical-role.html.

Lord and connection with His Spirit, confirming that they belong in our family and in the family of God. Whether in a formal ordinance or in common, everyday interactions, women and men can use friendly, appropriate touch to empower others' feelings of belonging and identity.

7. Pray for the sick in the name of Christ. The one priesthood ordinance that is neither recorded on the records of the Church nor requires specific permission is blessing the sick, and by extension other personal blessings. The Doctrine and Covenants does not specify giving blessings as a duty of the office of elder, but the scriptures do invite members who are sick to turn to the "elders" to "pray for and lay their hands upon them in my name" (D&C 42:44), "anointing him with oil in the name of the Lord" (James 5:14).

The prerogative of offering blessings of healing and guidance can feel to women like a lost gift, since women in the Church shared in this privilege into the early 1900s and could stand in the circle in giving such blessings even toward the end of the last century.[11] Personally, I would love to have been one of those women,

---

11. From President Joseph F. Smith: "A wife does not hold the priesthood in connection with her husband, but she enjoys the benefits thereof with him; and if she is requested to lay hands on the sick with him, or with any other officer holding the Melchizedek priesthood, she may do so with perfect propriety. It is no uncommon thing for a man and wife unitedly to administer to their children, and the husband being mouth, he may properly say out of courtesy, 'By authority of the holy priesthood in us vested'" (Joseph F. Smith, "Questions and Answers," *Improvement Era* [February 1907], 308–9. Reiterated and quoted by Joseph Fielding Smith, *Answers to Gospel Questions, Vol. 1*, [Salt Lake City; Deseret Book, 1979], 149–50).

Even more recently, from the life of Camilla Eyring Kimball, wife of President Spencer W. Kimball, as recorded by their son Edward: "Dad had just been given some codeine for headache; he had not said much according to the nurse, but he had asked for a blessing. . . . Pres. Benson was taking a treatment at the Deseret Gym and could not come right away, so the security man had called Elders McConkie and Hanks; Mother was glad. Elder Hanks anointed Dad and Elder McConkie sealed the anointing as I joined them. At Elder McConkie's suggestion Mother also placed her hands on Dad's head. That was unusual; it seemed right to me, but I would not have felt free to suggest it on my own because of an ingrained sense that the ordinance is a priesthood ordinance

but I am grateful that James goes on to assure, "And the prayer of faith shall save the sick. . . . Pray one for another, that ye may be healed. The effectual fervent prayer of a righteous man availeth much" (James 5:15–16). Women certainly share in the privilege of "pray[ing] for one another, that ye may be healed," with the promise that our "effectual fervent prayer" can "save the sick" and avail "much." Even though at this time only Melchizedek Priesthood bearers are authorized to use laying on of hands outside of the temple, I know from experience that women can pray for the sick and needy with power and can be heard.

Joseph Smith particularly admonished those giving priesthood blessings in his day to not administer these priesthood forms without priesthood power. According to Parley P. Pratt, during one period of great sickness in the Church, Joseph Smith personally healed many and "rebuked the Elders who would continue to lay hands on the sick . . . without the power to heal them. Said he: 'It is time that such things ended. *Let the Elders either obtain the power of God to heal the sick or let them cease to minister the forms without the power.*'"[12]

Yet apparently even Joseph Smith had to grow in the spiritual healing power he later became so proficient at. Five years before he performed these healing miracles and chastised others for ministering the forms without the power, he, Hyrum, and others fell violently ill with cholera at Zion's Camp: "Soon after arriving at the point of destination, the cholera broke out among us, and the brethren were so violently attacked that it seemed impossible to

---

(though I recalled Joseph Smith's talking of mothers blessing their children). After the administration Mother wept almost uncontrollably for some minutes, gradually calming down." https://www.lds.org/topics/joseph-smiths-teachings-about-priesthood-temple-and-women?lang=eng, footnote 32, Jonathan A. Stapley and Kristine Wright, "Female Ritual Healing in Mormonism," *Journal of Mormon History* 37, no. 1 (Winter 2011), 84.

12. *Autobiography of Parley P. Pratt,* Scott Facer Proctor and Maurine Jensen Proctor, eds. (Salt Lake City: Deseret Book, 2000), 355; emphasis in original.

render them any assistance. They immediately sent for [Hyrum and me] to lay hands on them, but . . . when we laid our hands upon them . . . , the disease instantly fastened itself upon us. And in a few minutes we were in awful distress."

Joseph and Hyrum's prayers and healing administrations to each other did not help.

"Hyrum cried out, 'Joseph what shall we do? Must we be cut off from the face of the earth by this horrid curse?' Joseph replied, 'Let us get down upon our knees and pray to God to remove the cramp and other distress and restore us to health, that we may return to our families.' . . . I cried heartily unto God, but the heavens seemed sealed against us and every power that could render us any assistance shut within its gates. The universe was still." They continued to pray. Finally, Hyrum exclaimed, "I have had an open vision, in which I saw mother on her knees under an apple tree praying for us, and she is even now asking God, in tears, to spare our lives. . . . The Spirit testifies to me that her prayers and ours shall be heard." *And from that moment, they were healed and went on their way rejoicing.*[13]

Joseph declared on his return, "Oh, my Mother! how often have your prayers been a means of assisting us when the shadows of death encompassed us!"[14]

Was Joseph and Hyrum's mother, Lucy Mack Smith, one whose faith and hope tutored them in obtaining the priesthood power Joseph later exercised with such confidence and chastised others for not having? This is an empowering story for women, mothers, and men alike. It is a testament that, as James assures us in the scripture quoted above, "the effectual fervent prayer of a righteous man [*or woman*] availeth much."

---

13. Lucy Mack Smith, *History of Joseph Smith by His Mother*, compiled by R. Vernon Ingleton (Provo, UT: Stratford Books), 336–38; emphasis in original.
14. Smith, *History of Joseph Smith by His Mother*, 338.

PRIESTHOOD POWER THROUGH PRIESTHOOD RESPONSIBILITIES

A personal experience with the power available to women of faith occurred when a dear family friend was diagnosed with breast cancer some thirty years ago. Especially because she had young children at home, her great desire was to be healed, but her cancer was so advanced that unproven, experimental treatments were her only medical hope. She decided to gather with friends who could pray together on her behalf. We gathered at my home, fasting, some of our husbands present as well. We talked of our love for her and our hope in God. When I was asked to say the prayer, I felt keenly my responsibility to not offer false hope but to pray with faith as inspired by the Holy Ghost.

The only way I can describe what I experienced as I prayed is to compare it to reading a teleprompter that scrolls through a script. I didn't see or hear words, but one at a time there came to my mind clear spiritual impressions, which I attempted to articulate. First were impressions about the Lord's great love for this friend, and then impressions about her children and other issues unrelated to her illness, each coming line upon line. Eventually impressions came to bless her that she would be completely healed. Frankly, I was less prepared to say those words than to offer consolation that she would not be, but I said what I felt impressed to say. When no more impressions came, I ended in the name of Jesus Christ. I have never experienced anything else quite like it.

My dear friend was the beneficiary of many priesthood blessings, state-of-the-art medical care, necessary surgery, and the faithful service and love of many people. She demonstrated great personal faith, including the faith to be healed and the faith to die. But I believe our "effectual fervent prayers" on her behalf contributed to her healing and the complete remission of her cancer. At the same time, this experience tutored us.

The Apostle Paul reminds us that even though we may struggle to put words to our impressions or feelings as we pray, the Spirit can tutor and intercede for us. He writes, "Likewise the Spirit also helpeth our infirmities [our mortal weakness]: for we know not what we should pray for as we ought: but the Spirit itself maketh intercession for us with groanings [Greek: sighings] which cannot be uttered" (Romans 8:26). This was my experience.

At one point during the visit of Jesus Christ to the Americas, His followers also prayed "without ceasing . . . and they did not multiply many words, for it was given unto them what they should pray, and they were filled with desire" (3 Nephi 19:24). When someone is taught by the Spirit what to pray for, he or she "asketh in the Spirit . . . according to the will of God; wherefore it is done even as he asketh" (D&C 46:30). When we are not sure what God's will is, even after fasting and prayer, we can still ask according to our desires and hopes, always affirming our submission to His desires and hopes for us.

Dana, a former Relief Society president who served our ward with incredible faith and spiritual sensitivity, was diagnosed a few years ago with stage four lung cancer that had metastasized to her brain, bones, and organs. Two of Dana's closest friends suggested a large group of her ward sisters gather to plan and to pray. In Dana's absence we discussed immediate family needs; we made plans and took assignments to help. Then one person was asked by Dana's closest friend to lead us in prayer. We each told her things we would personally like her to include, and she wrote them down to include according to her own inspiration, looking at the list periodically as she prayed. We considered our prayer a commitment to act.

Dana received many miracles over the next few years, including at one point being told against all odds that her illness was in remission. She saw a daughter depart on a mission and return. Another daughter announced a pregnancy and had a daughter of her own. Dana had the opportunity, despite being in a lot of pain, to travel to poor areas of South America to conduct teacher training she had been preparing and planning for years to deliver. She literally and figuratively danced in the rain.

When the cancer returned with a vengeance, a small group of her close friends gathered again to pray. This time she joined us and expressed her desires and her great faith. We talked about her family, the miracles she had received, and medical advances on the cusp of being able to help her. This time we knelt together, and each took a turn praying. We pleaded with God that His healing miracles would continue. We also prayed that His will would be done and that she and her family would be sustained no matter what happened. I believe that her life was prolonged because of this and many other prayers and priesthood blessings on her behalf.

The final gathering for this dear sister occurred a few months later as her husband and three daughters gathered in her hospital room and prayed her home to God.

I am reminded that all of the people Jesus Christ cured eventually died from something. All of our cures are temporary, and they will never be complete until the Resurrection. Being healed is different from being cured, however. Even if we are physically completely cured, illness can scar the heart, as can other experiences that leave us feeling separated from God. But when our "heart is waxed gross," and our "ears are dull of hearing" and our "eyes . . . closed," if we can "be converted," Christ stands ready to heal us (Matthew 13:15). *Even when we are not cured*, we can find great healing of what most ails us as we return to the Savior and become converted to a deeper and more abiding trust in Him. Conversion puts us in the path of His healing: "O all ye that are spared . . . will ye not now return unto me, and repent of your sins, and be converted, that I may heal you?" (3 Nephi 9:13).

Healing may involve feelings of peace, comfort, hope, or perspective. It may come from forgiving or from receiving a heartfelt and sensitive apology. It may come from seeing our own story in a new light. It may come from recognizing options we had not seen before, gaining the perspectives of eternity, or feeling surrounded by love and care, perhaps from both sides of the veil. These and many other forms of healing are blessings women can facilitate and provide.[15]

MANY WAYS TO HEAL

I gratefully note that Jesus Christ both cured and healed people in many ways, and seldom using what we would recognize as formal priesthood blessings. He touched the hand of Peter's mother-in-law and her fever left her (see Matthew 8:15). He "cast out the spirits with his word" for those possessed (Matthew 8:16). People who could but "touch the hem of his garment" were made whole (Matthew 14:36; 9:20–22). He used dirt and spit on the eyes of one who was blind (see John 9:14), touched the ears or tongue to restore hearing and speech (see John 9:14; Mark 7:33), and spit on a blind man's eyes and repeatedly put his hands on him until he saw clearly (see Mark 8:23–25). He simply declared that people be made whole, either speaking to them directly (see Luke 5:24) or without even seeing or touching them at all (see Matthew 8:13).

---

15. "Healing is a different process from cure. Healing involves a spiritual and emotional reweaving of our life story to incorporate, not merely revoke, our injuries. It involves growth and personal change, maturation into a new state of deeper trust in God despite, not in the absence of, suffering. It includes acceptance of our lost innocence, while reaching toward greater wisdom. Healing does not mean going back to Eden but going forward through the wounding world of mortality to a wholeness that transcends rather than excludes evil. While we cannot expect the temple to *cure* all our mortal ills, returning us to what we were before, it can help us *heal* from all our ills as God comforts, redeems, and changes us into something we have never been. The temple helps us regain momentum and direction when we become paralyzed. It offers relief and calm when our hearts race amid life's challenges. It teaches us of God's most powerful healing promises: forgiveness, sanctification, resurrection, and redemption. We can begin to access these healing promises today, even if cure must wait for tomorrow" (Wendy Ulrich, *The Temple Experience: Passage to Healing and Holiness* [Springville, Utah: Cedar Fort, 2009], 8–9).

And, sometimes, He "laid his hands upon" people to heal them as elders do today (Mark 6:5; Luke 13:13).

His disciples also healed in many ways. They laid hands on the sick (see Acts 28:8); they simply spoke to them in the name of Christ and then took them by the hand and lifted them up (see Acts 3:6–7); or they anointed them with oil and healed them (see Mark 6:13). The Old Testament records additional ways that people were healed, such as by dipping themselves in the Jordan River seven times at the word of a prophet (see 2 Kings 5:14) or looking on a brass serpent (see Numbers 21:8).

When Joseph Smith was unavailable to give his wife Emma a priesthood blessing, he invited her to write down the blessing she desired and he signed it. Just as a temple prayer of dedication or rededication is written down, some of the blessings we seek are important enough to think through and commit to writing and ask the Lord to bless. Similarly, when I go to the Lord in prayer with paper and pencil in hand, ready to write down impressions that might come, I more often receive more help and healing.

Women also use their healing gifts to speak words of comfort or guidance by the Spirit, to provide service in times of sickness or despair, to take over necessary tasks, to bathe or hold or touch the afflicted, and in many other ways to be the hands of God among His people.

Women are also essential and invited to circles of faith on behalf of those we pray to have healed. When participating in communal prayers, we sometimes *say* a prayer, or *hear* a prayer, and sometimes in either role we actually, truly pray when we focus and bring faith to the experience. I hope we bring as much private preparation to the privilege of being the voice of a public prayer as we want our brethren to bring to their privileges as we each try to obtain and articulate for others the will of the Lord as we pray.

Women in the early days of the Church, including after the

exodus to Utah, routinely gathered to anoint and bless women preparing to give birth.[16] While that practice has been discontinued, could we not gather close, righteous women friends to gather and pray with and for us as we anticipate the birth of a child or an impending adoption, or to mourn with us the absence of such experiences? I remember well the lonely hours of labor and can well imagine that the faith and companionship of women experienced in that process would have comforted me. I also wonder if women who have not given birth or who may not have that experience in this life might feel more included in the maternal circle if invited to, or convening, such an event.

All these examples remind me that there are many ways to participate in the gift and power of healing. Moroni's reminder that all spiritual gifts, including healing, are administered in different ways seems apt: "I would exhort you that ye deny not the power of God; for he worketh by power, according to the faith of the children of men, the same today and tomorrow, and forever. And again, I exhort you, my brethren, that ye deny not the gifts of God, for they are many; and they come from the same God. And there are different ways that these gifts are administered; but it is the same God who worketh all in all" (Moroni 10:7–8).

Women can participate in healing in many "different ways."

LEARNING THE HEALER'S ART

Elder Quentin L. Cook speaks of the healing of a woman with an "issue of blood" who touched the hem of Jesus's robe as He walked through a large crowd (see Luke 8:43–48). Noticing that "virtue" had gone out of Him, He stopped to find her. Elder Cook teaches: "The root word for *virtue* could easily be interpreted as

---

16. See Jill Mulvay Derr, Carol Cornwall Madsen, Kate Holbrook, Matthew J. Grow, eds., *The First Fifty Years of Relief Society: Key Documents in Latter-day Saint Women's History* (Salt Lake City: Church Historian's Press, 2016), 539.

'power.' In Spanish and Portuguese, it is translated as 'power.' But regardless, the Savior did not see her; He had not focused on her need. But her faith was such that touching the border of the garment drew upon the healing power of the Son of God."[17]

Although He did not lay hands on this woman's head, Christ's very body responded to her unidentified need and her exemplary faith with an outpouring of healing power. A woman elicited this healing blessing from Him—a woman who had been powerless on her own to find the healing she sought, a woman who was bleeding and thus "unclean." We as women can learn something about how power and healing can be administered, and claimed, from this story. We too as women (or as men) can develop the kind of faith that will draw power from Christ to heal us—whether or not He provides a cure. The gift of healing is not limited to the power to heal others; it also includes the gift of being healed.

Elder Cook further reminds us that practice, righteousness, and sustained personal growth are necessary to develop such enduring faith: "One . . . research expert asserts 'that ten thousand hours of practice is required to achieve the level of mastery associated with being a world-class expert—in anything.'[18]

"Most people recognize that to obtain peak physical and mental performance, such preparation and practice are essential.

"Unfortunately, in an increasingly secular world, less emphasis is placed on the amount of spiritual growth necessary to become more Christlike and establish the foundations that lead to enduring faith. . . . We do this by consecrated commitment to sacred sacrament meetings, scripture study, prayer, and serving as called."[19]

If I had my choice of spiritual gifts, healing would be high on my list. Out of that desire, I trained as a psychologist, praying that

---

17. Quentin L. Cook, "Foundations of Faith," *Ensign*, May 2017.
18. Daniel Levitin, quoted in Malcolm Gladwell, *Outliers: The Story of Success* (Boston: Little, Brown and Company, 2008), 40.
19. Cook, "Foundations of Faith."

the Lord would help me magnify that training with spiritual discretion and power. I still remember one of my very first clients—a dear sister who struggled with debilitating anxiety as well as spiritual concerns. I knew her stake president had given her a blessing, and as I realized the extent of her challenges and my own inexperience, I frankly wished that I too could just give her a blessing and be done. Instead we worked together for years to help her receive the blessing she had already been promised. She was not cured, but the Spirit provided many moments of healing that restored her to faith and hope even if they did not turn the off switch on her anxiety. I learned that the gifts of healing or being healed sometimes require great patience, skill, humility, and effort as we mourn together, comfort one another, bear one another's burdens, and testify of Christ.

So I will say with Alma, "I ought to be content with the things which the Lord hath allotted unto me. . . . Why should I desire more than to perform the work to which I have been called?" (Alma 29:3, 6). I too want to be content with the incomparable blessings I, as a woman, have received from God: power to be heard by God; power to receive and to act with the Holy Ghost; power to receive healing through faith on the Healer; power to bless, confirm, order, lead, preach, and, in the name of Christ, to access His healing power for others. I must never forget, however, that He is the Healer, and we are only the borrowers, powerless on our own.

EFFECTUAL FERVENT PRAYER

Without question, wives and children are blessed and supported in their individual missions when husbands and fathers grow in righteous priesthood power. President Russell M. Nelson has also taught, however: "We need women who know how to make important things happen by their faith and who are courageous defenders of morality and families in a sin-sick world. We need women who are devoted to shepherding God's children along the covenant path toward exaltation, women who know how to receive personal revelation, who understand the power and peace of the temple endowment, women who know how to call upon the powers of heaven to protect and strengthen children and families, women who teach fearlessly."[20]

We *do* need women of power as a Church, and I need to see powerful women to become one myself. We all, male and female, need mentoring, experience, and the opportunity to learn from both failure and success as we grow in such spiritual power.

As a mental health professional, as a temple worker, as a friend, as a woman, and in personal and intimate ways I have been privileged to represent holy messengers in petitioning the Lord on behalf of His children and bringing them to the gate of His presence. I have been blessed with the ministering of angels, angels on both sides of the veil, and with the wondrous influence and healing presence of the Father, Son, and Holy Ghost. I hold these experiences sacred. And I am trying to prepare for more.

---

20. Russell M. Nelson, "A Plea to My Sisters," *Ensign,* November 2015.

Chapter 8

GOVERN WITH POWER AND COMPASSION

HIGH PRIEST, BISHOP

No power or influence can or ought to be maintained by virtue of the priesthood, only by persuasion, by long-suffering, by gentleness and meekness, and by love unfeigned; By kindness, and pure knowledge, which shall greatly enlarge the soul without hypocrisy, and without guile. . . . Let thy bowels also be full of charity towards all men, and to the household of faith, and let virtue garnish thy thoughts unceasingly; then shall thy confidence wax strong in the presence of God; and the doctrine of the priesthood shall distil upon thy soul as the dews from heaven. The Holy Ghost shall be thy constant companion, and thy scepter an unchanging scepter of righteousness and truth; and thy dominion shall be an everlasting dominion, and without compulsory means it shall flow unto thee forever and ever.

DOCTRINE AND COVENANTS 121:41–42, 45–46

While walking down a church hallway during Primary, a counselor in the Primary presidency noticed eleven-year-old Scott wandering around. She stopped to talk to him, and through gentle questions learned that he "hated" his Primary class and had been wandering the halls during Primary for several weeks. She helped him get to class anyway, but then she found the Primary president,

PRIESTHOOD POWER THROUGH PRIESTHOOD RESPONSIBILITIES

> **DUTIES OF THE OFFICE OF HIGH PRIEST**
> - "Officiate . . . in administering spiritual things" (D&C 107:10)
> - "Officiate in the office of bishop . . . provided he is called and set apart and ordained" (v. 17)
> - "Settling important difficulties which might arise in the church" (D&C 102:2)
> - "Administer the everlasting gospel . . . [and] bring as many as will come to [it]" (D&C 77:11)

Sister Andrus, and told her about the situation. As they talked, they realized the boy's only friend in the class had graduated from Primary a month before, leaving Scott squirming in a room full of girls. They discussed several options and finally wondered if they could have Scott attend Sunday School with the twelve-year-olds and just come to Primary for sharing time. They talked to the bishopric counselor over Primary, and he concurred. Sister Andrus found Scott's mom (his dad wasn't there that day) to see what she thought. Mom appreciated the Primary leaders' sensitivity to a problem she had not been aware of. She was comfortable with the option they had come up with.

Sister Andrus got Scott out of class and invited him to a room to talk with her and his mom. Scott looked pretty nervous—he obviously thought he was in trouble—but Sister Andrus reassured him that nobody wanted him to have a bad experience at church and that they wanted to help. She and his mom explained the option they were thinking about and asked his opinion. He had some questions, which they addressed. He worried others might think it was weird for him to do church this way, but he did think it would help.

Sister Andrus said she knew Heavenly Father wanted Scott to be happy at church, and she asked if the three of them could pray together to ask Heavenly Father's confirmation on this decision. Sister Andrus invited Scott's mom to say the prayer, but, feeling somewhat emotional, his mom asked Sister Andrus to be the voice in their prayer. Sister Andrus thanked Heavenly Father for Scott and explained his situation. She expressed her love and his mother's love for Scott and their conviction that God loved Scott. She laid out the plan they had thought through and asked for a confirmation on their decision if it was good.

That confirmation came immediately. The Spirit was so strong that Sister Andrus was sure Scott and his mom could feel it too.

> **DUTIES OF THE OFFICE OF BISHOP**
>
> - "Administering all temporal things" (D&C 107:68)
> - "Be a judge in Israel" (v. 72)
> - "Do the business of the church" (v. 72)
> - "Sit in council with [the priests quorum], to teach them the duties of their office" (v. 87)

After she concluded the prayer, she asked Scott and his mom about their thoughts and feelings. Mom nodded, teary. Scott said he felt good. The plan was put into place.

I love this true story of women, acting under priesthood authority and with priesthood power, seeing a need within their stewardship, talking with the person they want to help, creating an option, counseling with the bishopric member and the parent, discussing the option with the individual in need, and praying together for spiritual confirmation. This is a wonderful example of an honest child, righteous Church leaders (female and male), a loving parent, and the Spirit of God working together to bless not only a hurting boy but everyone involved.

High priests and bishops are offices in the Melchizedek Priesthood particularly charged with the responsibility of leadership and governance (see the inset at the start of this chapter). High priests specifically administer the spiritual work of the Church, and they may be called to serve on a stake high council or stake presidency; to leadership in a bishopric or elders quorum; to oversee missions and ward missionary work, temples, and temple work; or to other roles of spiritual leadership.

Bishops administer the temporal work of the Church. A bishop ensures the temporal needs of his ward members are met; oversees the work of the Aaronic Priesthood and counsels the priests quorum; and serves as the "father" or "overseer" of the ward, with keys to administer all Church programs in the ward. In addition, the bishop is set apart as the presiding high priest in the ward, so he oversees the spiritual work of the ward, serves as a judge in Israel, and counsels with members to settle "important difficulties" among members and in families. These weighty roles require great personal and family sacrifice on behalf of the wards and stakes they serve.

Under the keys of these priesthood leaders, women are also authorized to fill a wide variety of leadership and governance roles in wards and stakes, in missions and in temples, in homes and in communities, both spiritually and temporally. You might ponder the responsibilities that attend all of these leadership roles and how you could appropriately sustain these men and women leaders and help carry their load. For now, let's explore specifically how the Lord's governance system of councils helps us all become more trustworthy in leadership roles and how we might more effectively participate in Church governance through councils.

PARADOXES OF POWER

President Russell M. Nelson has taught: "It is a remarkable blessing to serve in the Lord's true and living Church with His authority and power. The restoration of the priesthood of God, including the keys of the priesthood, opens to worthy Latter-day Saints the greatest of all spiritual blessings. We see those blessings flowing to women, men, and children throughout the world.

"We see faithful women who understand the power inherent in their callings and in their endowment and other temple ordinances. These women know how to call upon the powers of heaven to protect and strengthen their husbands, their children, and others they love. These are spiritually strong women who lead, teach, and minister fearlessly in their callings with the power and authority of God![1] How thankful I am for them!

"Likewise, we see faithful men who live up to their privileges as bearers of the priesthood. They lead and serve by sacrifice in the Lord's way with love, kindness, and patience. They bless, guide, protect, and strengthen others by the power of the priesthood they hold. They bring miracles to those they serve while they keep their own marriages and families safe. They shun evil and are mighty elders in Israel.[2] I am most thankful for them!"[3]

"Power or influence" (D&C 121:41) is a spiritual privilege, and it is also a temporal skill. Dacher Keltner, a psychology professor at the University of California, Berkeley, studies how the power of influence is gained and lost. In his book *The Power Paradox*,[4] Keltner cites research indicating that people who rise to power in many settings generally do so because they are enthusiastic and bold, kind and appreciative, focused and articulate about the task at hand, calm during times of stress, open to others' perspectives, assertive but humble, and focused on advancing the greater good.[5] The highest-performing business teams have leaders who are compassionate, ask questions, actively listen and empathize, tactfully use silence to make space for others to speak, avoid interrupting, invite the less powerful to express opinions, and consciously and frequently express gratitude.[6] The most influential leaders are good

---

1. See Russell M. Nelson, "A Plea to My Sisters," *Ensign* or *Liahona*, November 2015, 96 (reference in original).
2. See Russell M. Nelson, "The Price of Priesthood Power," *Ensign* or *Liahona*, May 2016, 66–69; see also Alma 13:7–8; Doctrine and Covenants 84:17–20, 35–38 (reference in original).
3. Russell M. Nelson, "Ministering with the Power and Authority of God," *Ensign*, May 2018.
4. Dacher Keltner, *The Power Paradox: How We Gain and Lose Influence* (New York: Penguin Press, 2016).
5. See Keltner, *The Power Paradox*, 50.
6. See Keltner, *The Power Paradox*, 76–89.

storytellers who help create a cohesive narrative about projects, goals, and lessons from both failure and success.[7]

Keltner notes that these skills, and the team performance they facilitate, rise in groups as the proportion of women rises at the table.[8] To be blunt, a lot of women already excel in these leadership and governance skills, and men or women who lack these skills can learn them. Sometimes women just don't recognize that these skills qualify them to lead or participate in Church governance in helpful and meaningful ways.

Keltner concluded from his research that once people have attained power, however—and this is the paradox—both men and women in business leadership roles tend to shift their attention away from others to focus on selfish desires and interests. In other words, the very skills and attitudes that bring people to power in business settings often fade into the background once power is attained. Keltner found that once people rise to power they tend to become more self-serving, impulsive, disrespectful, and impolite. Their stories shift away from empathy for others' problems to tales of their own exceptional worth or deserving. Their ability to read and be moved by others' emotions declines.[9] Even people *artificially and temporarily* assigned a role of power in a social science experiment were more likely than their previous equals to grab the last cookie or talk with their mouth full, impulsively ignoring social politeness.[10] Contrary to popular opinion, the more powerful and well-off are *more* likely to shoplift than the poor and disadvantaged,[11] and those who have been primed to feel powerful are more likely to endorse things like speeding, over-reporting

---

7. See Keltner, *The Power Paradox*, 93.
8. See Keltner, *The Power Paradox*, 76.
9. See Keltner, *The Power Paradox*, 101–3, 109, 115.
10. See Keltner, *The Power Paradox*, 117–18.
11. See Keltner, *The Power Paradox*, 127.

travel expenses, or not paying taxes, even while condemning others for doing so.[12]

The Lord is prophetic about these findings, warning, "It is the nature and disposition of almost all men [and women], as soon as they get a little authority as they suppose [to] immediately begin to exercise unrighteous dominion," to cover sins, gratify pride and vain ambition, persecute the saintly, and fight against God (D&C 121:37–39). These warnings apparently apply to us all, male and female, in and out of Church settings. Powerful leaders can do much good, but powerful leaders motivated by self-interest and without morality or the Spirit can also inflame hatred, get the wrong things done, and unleash destruction and sorrow.

Even "telestial" command and control leaders may help people respond effectively and quickly to an emergency. Sound "terrestrial" leadership principles developed through good social science and solid experience provide a strong foundation for good leadership. "Celestial" leadership principles add a holy purpose and spiritual tools essential to good governance in the Church and kingdom of God.

The Doctrine and Covenants tutors us in the principles by which we increase in "celestial" priesthood power: "Power or influence can or ought to be maintained by virtue of the priesthood, only by persuasion, by long-suffering, by gentleness and meekness, and by love unfeigned; by kindness, and pure knowledge, which shall greatly enlarge the soul without hypocrisy, and without guile" (D&C 121:41–42).

HAVE CONFIDENCE IN COUNCILS

Excellence in anything that requires a team effort does not depend on one shining star but on the effectiveness of the group.

---

12. Keltner, *The Power Paradox*, 120, 131.

A large international business study found that the performance of a business function's *team* predicted the success of the overall business four to one over the performance of individual talent.[13] In both sports and film, the highest-ranked individuals are only on the winning team or film about twenty percent of the time.[14] Governance in the Church is also most effective when it makes effective use of councils. Although we often think of revelation for the Church as coming to a prophet alone on a mountaintop or a leader in solitary prayer, much of the revelation and practical planning we need to lead and govern at Church and at home comes as we gather in councils, presidencies, families, and other group settings.[15]

Our confidence in the power of councils increases when we have 1) skills to participate effectively in councils; 2) confidence in the value of diversity in councils; 3) confidence in our contributions to councils; and 4) confidence in the Lord's willingness to inspire councils. Let's look at these points in more detail.

1. Skills to participate effectively in councils. It has taken me some time to appreciate the value of councils. They can feel cumbersome and frankly frustrating at times. It is easy to feel irrelevant and tune out when I am just one of many voices and progress is slow. Apparently I am not alone. Elder Dale G. Renlund and Sister Ruth Lybbert Renlund begin a discussion of councils by quoting Joseph Smith: "In ancient days councils were conducted with such strict propriety that no one was allowed to whisper, be weary, leave

---

13. See Dave Ulrich, David Kryscynski, Mike Ulrich, and Wayne Brockbank, *Victory through Organization: Why the War for Talent is Failing your Company and What You Can Do about It* (New York: McGraw Hill, 2017).
14. My husband, Dave, did a quick analysis of how many times the team with the Most Valuable Player for a given league also won the national championship in recent years and how often the Academy Award winner for best actor or actress was also in the film that won best picture.
15. See M. Russell Ballard, "Strength in Council," *Ensign*, October 1993; "Counseling with our Councils," *Ensign*, April 1994; "Family Councils," *Ensign*, April 2016.

the room, or get uneasy in the least . . . but in our councils, generally, one will be uneasy, another asleep, . . . one's mind on the business of the council, and another thinking on something else."[16]

Wouldn't you love to know how Joseph Smith learned about councils in "ancient days" where people never got weary or uneasy? As I think about councils I'm a part of at home or at church, it is helpful to measure myself against nine characteristics or tasks of effective council participants described by Elder and Sister Renlund:

- Set goals focused on ministering to the welfare of souls, not on superficial issues.
- Offer your respective organization's resources for helping the whole rather than lobbying for your own organization's agenda or needs.
- Prepare ahead so you can report on past assignments, contribute to the discussion, bring the Spirit, and listen for direction.
- Focus on problem-solving around a few specific items, minimizing announcements, calendaring, or superficial discussions of too many items.
- Come on time, fully engage in the business at hand, avoid being distracted by side conversations or phones, actively contribute, and respectfully engage others with questions.
- Look for ways to help accomplish the work of the council and accept—even volunteer for—assignments rather than avoid them.
- Look for ways to use locally generated statistics to inform local decisions; seek out the concerns of the individuals behind the numbers.
- Focus on making decisions, helping all members of the council contribute to and fully support decisions made.

---

16. Joseph Smith, in *Teachings of the Prophet Joseph Smith*, comp. Joseph Fielding Smith (1976), 69.

- Anticipate and notice revelation as a result of counseling together, praying together, and your personal inspiration.[17]

One especially effective tool council participants often overlook is building on comments of others. Many good ideas brought forward in councils are never pursued because nobody "seconds the motion" by agreeing, asking questions, giving another example, or in other ways supporting the first person's concern or idea. Effective council participants can move the business of a council forward dramatically by noticing good ideas and providing a "second witness" that keeps the idea on the table and moving forward.

These principles remind women and men alike that effective councils almost always invite and even require the full participation of many, rather than depending on the authoritative decision of one.

2. Confidence in the value of diversity in councils. Councils are most effective when diverse viewpoints are represented. Elder Melvin J. Ballard teaches that, for openers, the diverse viewpoints of priesthood leaders and sister leaders working together in councils can help both more effectively magnify priesthood power and bless lives: "Any priesthood leader who does not involve his sister leaders with full respect and inclusion is not honoring and magnifying the keys he has been given. His power and influence will be diminished until he learns the ways of the Lord.

". . . Ward and stake councils that are the most successful are those in which priesthood leaders trust their sister leaders and encourage them to contribute to the discussions and in which sister leaders fully respect and sustain the decisions of the council made under the direction of priesthood leaders who hold keys. Families are helped and individuals are activated through council

---

17. See Dale G. and Ruth Lybbert Renlund, *The Melchizedek Priesthood: Understanding the Doctrine, Living the Principles* (Salt Lake City: Deseret Book, 2018), 143–49.

meetings in which this partnership exists and in which the focus is on people."[18]

I especially appreciate the value of diverse voices in a council when I'm one of the "diversities" I hope will be included. But when I'm the leader, it can feel simpler to "keep my own counsel." I was therefore very interested in a social science experiment in which teams were given complex problems to solve. Half of the teams consisted of four friends. Half had three friends and a stranger. Not surprisingly, the four friends enjoyed the experience significantly more, were more confident that their solutions were solid, and got correct answers about fifty percent of the time—pretty good! The teams with the stranger in the mix, however, got the correct answers about seventy-five percent of the time. That's a fifty percent improvement in team performance by getting someone new to the group on board, even though it left those team members feeling less self-assured and having less fun.

Surprisingly, the newcomers *didn't even bring in new information*; their presence simply stimulated the team to think more outside the box and not jump to conclusions.[19] Other studies confirm the value of diversity in helping work teams be more factually accurate, more appropriately cautious, more innovative, and more values-driven.[20] In contrast, *groupthink* (coming to decisions too quickly because everyone agrees) is more likely to occur when the group overestimates its power or morality, doesn't question its own assumptions, doesn't seek out alternative viewpoints, negatively stereotypes outsiders who might disagree, and shields itself from

---

18. "Let Us Think Straight," BYU Education Week Devotional address, https://speeches.byu.edu/talks/m-russell-ballard_let-us-think-straight-2/.
19. See Katherine W. Phillips, Katie A. Liljenquist, Margaret A. Neale, "Is the Pain Worth the Gain? The Advantages and Liabilities of Agreeing with Socially Distinct Newcomers," *Personality and Social Psychology Bulletin*, Vol. 35, Issue 3 (2009), 336–50.
20. See David Rock and Heidi Grant, "Why Diverse Teams are Smarter," *Harvard Business Review* (2016), https://hbr.org/2016/11/why-diverse-teams-are-smarter.

internal conflict.[21] These are dangerous oversights for any homogenous group that ward or stake leadership councils or presidencies are wise to guard against.

Families or wards in which nearly everyone has always been an active Church member or a Republican or a BYU fan may enjoy a lot of unity, but families and wards that learn to value and learn from their internal differences bring great assets to the building of Zion. After all, Zion is defined as a place where unity has developed because there are "no poor among them," that is, because there is no one with nothing to offer to the good of the whole (Moses 7:18).

3. Confidence in our contributions to councils. Even if councils are well served by being diverse, many people do not feel confident about their ability to contribute effectively to a council.

Whether in or out of the Church, when most of the participants in a council setting are men, women can feel at a disadvantage. Men talking with just other men often use a different conversational style from women talking with other women, and those style differences can create misunderstanding for both.[22] When men talk with men, their conversational style often includes more interrupting, disagreeing, jockeying for hierarchical position, and emphasizing differences of opinion.[23] By contrast, women talking with women tend to focus more on similarities, interrupt more to agree or encourage, defer quickly if two people talk at once, avoid or smooth over conflict, and emphasize social connection.

Most people are not conscious of these different norms, and when people stick with their own gender they aren't a big problem.

---

21. See I. L. Janis, *Groupthink: Psychological Studies of Policy Decisions and Fiascoes* (Boston: Houghton Mifflin, 1982).
22. See Deborah Tannen, *You Just Don't Understand: Women and Men in Conversation* (New York: Ballentine, 1990).
23. See Christopher F. Karpowitz and Tali Mendelberg, *The Silent Sex: Gender, Deliberation & Institutions* (Princeton: Princeton University Press, 2015).

But in mixed groups, men's style can leave women feeling dismissed, ignored, and threatened—and it is important for women to realize this is not usually intended or even conscious. At the same time, while men will fight for airtime, women will tend to defer and stop talking, unintentionally setting themselves up to feel ignored and to blame men for the problem. (In fact, women *do* risk coming across as aggressive and unfeminine if they're too assertive, since both men and women are more prone to see assertive men as "effective leaders" but see equally assertive women as "domineering and pushy."[24]) A male BYU professor and a female Princeton professor who studied women's participation in groups conclude that only when women are in the clear majority in a group do they come close to talking as much or feeling as valued as men.[25]

Researchers conclude that one way of increasing women's voices is to insist on unanimity rather than majority rule.[26] Interestingly, this is the implicit standard in Church councils, starting with the highest councils of the First Presidency and the Quorum of the Twelve Apostles: "And every decision made by either of these quorums must be by the unanimous voice of the same; that is, every member in each quorum must be agreed to its decisions, in order to make their decisions of the same power or validity one with the other" (D&C 107:27).

The unanimity standard works to the advantage of less confident members of councils, and that often means women, as we will explore in a moment. However, the goal is not just to make the women feel better but to improve the effectiveness of the council itself, and these researchers conclude "that the number of women in the group substantially affects the group's ability to solve problems collectively." Why? Because what helps groups succeed is

---

24. Katty Kay and Claire Shipman (2014), *The Confidence Code: The Science and Art of Self-Assurance—What Women Should Know* (New York: Harper Collins), 95.
25. Kay and Shipman, *The Confidence Code*, 231.
26. Kay and Shipman, *The Confidence Code*, 171.

"equally distributed talk and a high average ability to empathize, both of which were produced by having lots of women. The implication of these results is that gender inequality matters not only for justice but also for the group's ability to solve problems accurately."[27] That's good to know.

When I was in high school I became convinced that male confidence was mostly hot air and that girls were simply more genuine. To prove my point, I once asked a bunch of my friends about this long, heavy wire I'd noticed extended along the ceiling at the back of our multipurpose cafeteria. When I asked a boy, "What's that wire along the ceiling back there?" he always had an answer, including things like, "Oh, they use that to hang banners for assemblies," or, "That's for hanging lights for the school plays," or, "It's an electrical cord for Christmas lights," or, "They used to have a curtain up there." These were all reasonable possibilities, but they weren't expressed as reasonable possibilities. They were expressed as facts, put forward with total confidence. Every single girl I asked would look at the wire, think for a minute, and then say, "I have no idea."

I no longer think all boys are just braggarts and all girls just honest. It may be that the boys I asked were just trying to be helpful and the girls were being intellectually lazy or were overly nervous about being wrong. But researchers do conclude pretty consistently that, on the whole, women are less confident than men.[28] Women are less likely to express opinions, especially in mixed-sex groups.[29] Women tend to underestimate their ability or talent, while men tend to overestimate how well they are doing, even when their actual performance is nearly identical.[30] Women

---

27. Kay and Shipman, *The Confidence Code*, 140–41.
28. See Kay and Shipman, *The Confidence Code*.
29. See Karpowitz and Mendelberg, *The Silent Sex*.
30. See Karpowitz and Mendelberg, *The Silent Sex*, 15, 17, 51–52; see also Katty Kay and Claire Shipman, "The Confidence Gap," *The Atlantic,* May 2014.

have a harder time than men rebounding from negative feedback, and even the possibility of negative feedback leads women to avoid opportunities to grow or contribute.[31] Women in difficult economics classes were much more likely to drop the class if their grades weren't stellar than men getting the same grades.[32] Women initiate salary negotiations only once or twice for every nine times men do,[33] and when women do ask for a raise, they ask for thirty percent less money than men ask for.[34] Women in one large corporation would apply for an in-house job change or promotion only when they thought they had one hundred percent of the requested experience or skills, while men would apply with just sixty percent of the experience or skills asked for.[35]

On average, men have both a social and a biological edge in confidence. For example, the average man has ten times more testosterone than the average woman, and that hormone is strongly associated with more risk-taking. (Wall Street traders given testosterone made riskier trades, and when their risks paid off, their testosterone increased even more, potentially leading to higher losses.[36]) As a result of testosterone, boys take on more muscle and height when they reach adolescence; while women do too, they also take on increased physical vulnerability to sexual assault and a heightened sense of vulnerability. The part of the brain some call the "worrywart" center is—you guessed it—larger in women, keeping them scanning for threats and imperfections that can heighten anxiety and undermine confidence.[37]

---

31. See Karpowitz and Mendelberg, *The Silent Sex*, 145.
32. See Claudia Goldin, "Gender and the Undergraduate Economics Major: Notes on the Undergraduate Economics Major at a Highly Selective Liberal Arts College" (2015), https://scholar.harvard.edu/files/goldin/files/claudia_gender_paper.pdf.
33. See Linda Babcock and Sara Laschever, *Women Don't Ask: Negotiation and the Gender Divide* (New York: Bantam Books, 2007), 1–2.
34. See Babcock and Laschever, *Women Don't Ask*.
35. See Kay and Shipman, *The Confidence Code*, 21.
36. See Kay and Shipman, *The Confidence Code*, 114–15.
37. See Kay and Shipman, *The Confidence Code*, 112–13.

Nevertheless, confidence is a skill we can learn, even if we're not swimming in testosterone. And confidence is a skill worth acquiring if women or men are to contribute more fully to the building of Zion as either participants or leaders of councils. Short of changing our biology, here are several things that can help:

Have a plan. Confidence increases when we go into a situation with a plan—a plan for living our values or practicing a skill instead of just trying to feel safe. For example, when participating in an ongoing council recently, I noticed how often I vacillated between wanting to demonstrate I had some legitimate expertise to justify my being there and wanting to not be seen as pushy or out of turn. I started thinking about my values in this situation and concluded I wanted to do more to "second" good suggestions of others, provide additional information from research or the scriptures, and ask more questions that might help move ideas forward. To remind me, I wrote on the top of my agenda when I walked in, "Build and ask." I didn't say a lot more during those next meetings than usual, but I contributed more to its effectiveness. I felt my "confidence wax strong[er]" when I was actively living my values of supporting, contributing, and being curious and not just playing it safe (D&C 121:45).

Other things I've included in my "confidence plan" at various times have been:

- Learn people's names and use them.
- Prepare ahead of time so I'm clear about what I want to bring up or report on.
- Don't whine about how busy I am or blame others for dropping the ball.
- Ask about the values, direction, and big-picture goals of the group so we don't get lost in the weeds.
- Ask often, "What's the decision we need to make? How soon? Whose decision is it?"

- Represent the needs of the whole and of other interest groups than mine.
- Be friendly, supportive, and compassionate.
- Listen for and then articulate, "It sounds to me like we have these options . . ."
- Express my opinions, experience, and perspectives (without dominating), even when others may push back.

When I've been the only woman in a group of men, I have made additional plans:

- Dress a little more formally if everyone else will be in a shirt and tie.
- Work hard to not be easily offended when I'm ignored or interrupted.
- If I am interrupted, be willing to hold up my hand and say, "Hang on, I'm not finished," with a smile and a light touch.
- Don't take on a secretarial role unless that's my assignment.
- Look everyone in the eye so they'll be more likely to look at me and see me too.
- Don't give up and withdraw (but don't talk the most either).
- When a question is asked or a problem posed, make the first comment sometimes.

Practice resilience. My friend Alicyn Wright's father taught her she could achieve anything she wanted if she wasn't afraid to fail. Alicyn has achieved so many of her goals by working extremely hard at what she does, *and* by not being intimidated by the possibility of failing. Learning not to fear failure may be one way boys get a leg up on girls in confidence. Young girls are better on average at being compliant, sitting quietly, and following rules than their roughhousing, more impulsive brothers, so more of their identity can get tied up from an early age with being good and pleasing, while boys get more practice with brushing off criticism. Even participating on sports teams, which men do much more consistently than women, gives men more practice with taking criticism in stride, leaning in to competition, and getting back in the game after missing the shot, getting behind, or losing completely.[38] In other words, *practicing failing and resilience is more important for confidence than practicing perfection.* As one researcher asserts, "Of all the warped things women do to themselves to undermine their confidence, we found the pursuit of perfection to be the most crippling."[39]

Carol Dweck, a professor at Stanford University who studies resilience, found that more resilient students didn't initially succeed more often than others, but they bounced back from failure more readily. In fact, they didn't even think they were failing. They just thought they were learning. They assumed that no matter how much or how little talent they had for something, they could improve quite a bit. Not doing well didn't mean they were stupid; it just meant they needed to practice more, get more help, or be more creative.[40]

Try that on for size. If that council you are part of isn't going well, or if your participation there isn't very effective yet, what if you're not failing? What if you're learning?

Tolerate anxiety. We don't have to eliminate anxiety to act with confidence. We just have to decide anxiety isn't the end of the world. I know this is a bit unconventional in a book directed to women, but let's broaden our traditional repertoire and consider a sports example! Bill Russell, a center for the Boston Celtics, was an NBA all-star twelve times (the record is thirteen), was Most Valuable Player of the year five times (the record is six), and won eleven NBA championships in his thirteen years as a professional basketball player, helping to make the Celtics the most winning basketball team in history. *And* before the start of most of these games, Bill Russell became so anxious he threw up. In fact, when

---

38. See Kay and Shipman, *The Confidence Code*, 88, 91.
39. Kay and Shipman, *The Confidence Code*, 106.
40. See Carol Dweck, *Mindset: The New Psychology of Success* (New York: Random House, 2006).

he finally got his anxiety under control enough to stop throwing up before games, he went into a serious losing streak that only ended when he started throwing up again. His teammates loved the sound of Bill throwing up in the locker room because they knew he'd have a great game. Confidence for Bill Russell didn't mean figuring out how to not throw up before stepping out with his team. It meant increasing his tolerance for anxiety and not seeing it as something embarrassing or in his way.[41]

Fortunately, then, women do not have a corner on anxiety. In fact, it sort of seems like Moroni, the great warrior-prophet of the Book of Mormon, was at one point almost immobilized with worry about his writing "weakness" and about the mocking of readers who wouldn't even be alive for 1500 years. At least the people that I worry will look down on me have actually been born! It apparently took a personal visit from the Savior to talk Moroni down, Christ assuring him that "fools mock, but . . . my grace is sufficient for all . . . that humble themselves before me . . . and have faith in me" (Ether 12:26–27). Eventually, Moroni leaves us with this fervent testimony: "I have seen Jesus, and . . . he hath talked with me face to face, and . . . he told me in plain humility, even as a man telleth another in mine own language, concerning these things" (v. 39). This humble, charitable, honest, and confident Jesus is of course the God of our salvation as women, too.

4. Confidence in the Lord's willingness to inspire councils—which underscores that the most important tool in our confidence toolbox as we step into councils is to trust God's confidence in us. I have learned that I can trust God, trust Him

---

41. For some people, anxiety is a debilitating disorder that is only nominally managed despite everything they try. Most of us, however, actually perform better when we are a little anxious. Ironically, anxiety and high intelligence tend to go hand in hand, and because anxious people tend to be more conscientious and hardworking, they are often more successful. So anxiety is unpleasant, but it is not necessarily a deal-breaker for accomplishment or for having an adequate level of confidence to succeed.

completely—not because He will always keep me safe or always hold my hand, but because He will always come back to comfort, teach, and redeem me. I have also learned—and this lesson has been even harder won—that God can trust me. Certainly that does not mean He can trust me to always be right, or perfect, or even confident. But I have seen over the decades that I, too, keep coming back. He and I can trust me to continue to try again.

It is instructive to me that most of the work of the Church at the highest levels takes place through councils, working over many years toward better and better solutions to complex problems. Even when a high-level Church council reaches its conclusions under the influence of prophetic revelation or individual inspiration, new programs are carefully tested, piloted, and refined before being implemented. This helps the Church avoid groupthink, consider a broader diversity of experience than that of a few council members, and seek better information that can lead to better inspiration. Even in individual decisions, we can benefit from counseling with others, testing our conclusions carefully and with openness to change, and getting better information that can lead to better inspiration.

There are many voices in our heads, chattering away about the looming opinions of others, the unsuitability of our skills, the impurity of our intent, or the unacceptability of our offerings. But the voice of the Lord will neither mock our efforts nor lack compassion for our fears. His is the still, small voice of plain humility and peace in which we can afford to place our confidence. As both men and women increase in personal righteousness, "The doctrine of the priesthood shall distil upon [our] soul as the dews from heaven" in our "dominions" of holy influence in the councils of the Church and the home. Our confidence can wax strong in His presence with us, and in our presence at the tables of leadership in His Church (D&C 121:45–46).

Chapter 9
BLESS THE RISING GENERATION
PATRIARCH, SEALER

[Isaiah] had reference to those whom God should call in the last days, who should hold the power of priesthood to bring again Zion, and the redemption of Israel; and to put on her strength is to put on the authority of the priesthood, which she, Zion, has a right to by lineage; also to return to that power which she had lost.

DOCTRINE AND COVENANTS 113:8

The priesthood office of a patriarch in the Melchizedek Priesthood was first held in this dispensation by Joseph Smith's father, Joseph Smith Sr., and then by Joseph's older brother Hyrum, the Assistant President of the Church (see D&C 124:91),[1] who was also given sealing power: "That from henceforth he shall hold the keys of the patriarchal blessings upon the heads of all my people, That whoever he blesses shall be blessed, and whoever he curses shall be cursed; that whatsoever he shall bind on earth shall be bound in heaven; and whatsoever he shall loose on earth shall be loosed in heaven. . . .

---

1. Fathers of large tribal families who also held priesthood authority to bless and govern were referred to in the Bible as patriarchs (see Acts 7:8–9; Hebrews 7:4). Peter was given the power to seal both on earth and in heaven by the Savior (see Matthew 16:19).

> **DUTIES OF THE OFFICE OF PATRIARCH**
>
> - "Hold the keys of the patriarchal blessings upon the heads of all my people" (D&C 124:92)

to hold the sealing blessings of my church, even the Holy Spirit of promise, whereby ye are sealed up unto the day of redemption, that ye may not fall notwithstanding the hour of temptation that may come upon you" (D&C 124:92–95, 124).

Patriarchs ensure that all members have the opportunity for a patriarchal blessing, which declares the person's primary lineage within the twelve tribes of Israel and pronounces words of blessing, guidance, warning, and prophecy. Patriarchs used to be ordained by a member of the Twelve, but they are now ordained by their stake president.

Related to the office of a patriarch is the sealing power. President Boyd K. Packer describes this power: "The sealing power represents the transcendent delegation of spiritual authority from God to man. The keeper of that sealing power is the Lord's chief representative here upon the earth, the President of the Church. . . .

"The keys of the sealing power are synonymous with the keys of the everlasting priesthood. . . . That sacred sealing power is with the Church now. Nothing is regarded with more sacred contemplation by those who know the significance of this authority. Nothing is more closely held. . . . Those keys—the keys to seal and bind on earth, and have it bound in heaven—represent the consummate gift from our God."[2]

We also learn from Elder James E. Talmage that "the patriarchal order of the priesthood is the organizing power and principle of celestial family life" and "the ideal form of government."[3] Within

---

2. Boyd K. Packer, *The Holy Temple* (Salt Lake City: Deseret Book, 1980), 82–83.
3. In *Encyclopedia of Mormonism, Vol. 3*, (New York: Macmillan Publishing, 1992) 1067. It also states, "To Latter-day Saints, the patriarchal order of the priesthood is the organizing power and principle of celestial family life. It is the ultimate and ideal form of government. . . . The highest order of the Melchizedek Priesthood

the patriarchal order, "woman shares with man the blessings of the Priesthood . . . cooperating to the full in the government of their family kingdom."[4] Temple sealers organize eternal families within this order. The power to seal families is given to each temple sealer directly by the President of the Church or an Apostle he specifically authorizes. While "sealer" is not a priesthood office, a sealer retains the sealing power throughout his life.[5]

> **DUTIES OF THE CALLING OF SEALER**
>
> - "Whatsoever he shall bind on earth shall be bound in heaven" (D&C 124:93)
> - "Sealing of the children to their parents" (D&C 138:48)

While relatively few men are patriarchs or temple sealers, both women and men share in many privileges associated with these offices, including the gift of prophecy to discern and complete our earthly mission, becoming patriarchs/matriarchs (parents) who raise the next generation spiritually or physically, participating in the sealing power, and empowering others in these roles. We'll especially consider how these privileges might apply to women.

DEVELOPING THE GIFTS OF REVELATION, VISION, AND PROPHECY

One of the privileges of ancient patriarchs was to bless their children and prophesy on their behalf (see Genesis 48:15–19). Patriarchs today make it possible for every worthy member of the Church to receive such a blessing, which is recorded on the official records of the Church. Elder John A. Widtsoe explains: "The patriarch, looking into the future, enumerates the blessings and

---

is patriarchal authority. The order was divinely established with father Adam and mother Eve. . . . The promises given to Abraham and Sarah pertain to this same order."

4. James E. Talmage, *Young Woman's Journal 25*, 602–3 (quoted in previous note).
5. Active patriarchs and sealers always function under the keys and supervision of a specific stake president or temple president, however.

promises, some special, others general, to which the person of the proper lineage . . . is entitled; and through his authority seals them upon him [or her], so that they may be his [or hers] forever through faithfulness."[6]

The power to prophesy for, counsel with, and bless our children with an expanded vision of who they are is also specifically extended to women, as exemplified in this story from President Henry B. Eyring: "The revelation of a parent has its lasting effect in the personal revelation that continues in the child.

"My mother must have understood that principle of revelation. As a young man, I would close the back door very quietly when I came home late in the evening. I had to pass my mother's bedroom on the way to mine. However quietly I tiptoed, just as I got to her half-opened door, I would hear my name, ever so quietly, 'Hal, come in for a moment.'

"I would go in and sit on the edge of her bed. The room would be dark. If you had listened, you would have thought it was only friendly talk about life. But to this day, what she said comes back to my mind with the same power I feel when I read the transcript of my patriarchal blessing.

"I don't know what she was asking for in prayer as she waited for me those nights. I suppose it would have been in part for my safety. But I am sure that she prayed as a patriarch does before he gives a blessing. He prays that his words will come to the recipient as the words of God, not his. My mother's prayers for that blessing were answered on my head. She is in the spirit world and has been for more than 40 years. I am sure she has been exceedingly glad that I was blessed, as she asked, to hear in her counsel the commands of God. And I have tried to go and do as she hoped I would."[7]

Two women, Elisabeth and Mary, were the first witnesses of

---

6. John A. Widtsoe, *Evidences and Reconciliations* (1943–51), 1:73–74.
7. Henry B. Eyring, "Continuing Revelation," *Ensign*, November 2014.

the imminent birth and redemptive role of Jesus Christ (just as women were the first witnesses of His Resurrection). President J. Reuben Clark notes the gift of revelation, vision, and prophecy in the words of Mary about her unborn son, Jesus Christ (see Luke 1:46–55): "The spirit of prophecy entered her soul, and, recalling the past, and being enlightened as to the future, she forecast the work and service, the love and character of him whom she was to bring forth—the Christ, the Redeemer of the World.

"So measurably may every mother who has lived and is living righteously, envision something of the destiny of her offspring, if it be God's will."[8]

I know many women who have been given glimpses of their children or grandchildren before they were born, including one with no children who saw herself in another realm amid a large gathering of children she had been assigned to raise and teach. I have seen such glimpses quite unexpectedly with one of my three children and two of my nine grandchildren, but not with all of them. In one case when I prayed with some concern for information about a grandchild to be born, I was specifically told by the Lord that her future was not mine to know but that I could be reassured that whatever happened, it was in His hands and all was proceeding according to plan. I have found that my prophetic glimpses into others' lives are generally something to be kept to myself and revealed, if at all, as a secondary witness. When such gifts come to us on behalf of those in our stewardship or dear to our hearts, it is always subject to their agency and receipt of confirmation. Righteous fathers may use their priesthood power to give each of their children a private patriarchal blessing in addition to the one recorded by the Church. Mothers or fathers in Israel can

---

8. J. Reuben Clark, "Our Wives and Our Mothers in the Eternal Plan," *Relief Society Magazine*, December 1946.

live up to our privilege to pray, fast, and prepare for the gifts of prophecy, revelation, and vision on behalf of our children.

The grandfather of a dear friend of mine was asked by his granddaughter, my friend's sister, to give her his very first blessing after becoming an ordained patriarch. He was deeply concerned about interjecting his own thoughts or desires for her into the blessing, but when he read the blessing as transcribed, he felt that he had "overcorrected," leaving out some inspired impressions he had received from the Lord. He asked his leaders what to do and was counseled to write an official addendum to the blessing to include the additional inspiration he had received but not originally voiced.[9] I'm so grateful to know that patriarchs, as well as parents and all of us, can grow into the principle of revelation and prophecy with practice and prayer.

COMPLETING AN INDIVIDUAL MISSION

A common element in many patriarchal blessings is a peek into the premortal world where we were foreordained to our personal mission in mortality. Patriarchal blessings give us glimpses of our personal mission that can strengthen our ability to fulfill it. I am eternally indebted to the patriarch whose revelatory blessing has helped shape my values and goals and accomplish my purpose.

In many ways, women have had as powerful a role as a patriarch in helping me grasp my work on earth. My mother, grandmothers, aunts, sister, children, grandchildren, and friends have been essential in shaping my understanding of my gifts, my earthly mission and potential, and my premortal identity.

For example, my wonderful Aunt Jan was married to my mother's brother, so we were not blood relatives. I was not in touch with her at all during one period of great struggle and adversity in

---

9. Personal correspondence.

my life, but later she told me of a vision she had had as she was vacuuming her living room rug one day—a vision that included information about her husband, his mother and sister, and even me. In her vision she saw something of my premortal identity, the process by which I was sent to my particular family, and the choosing of my mortal name. The fact that she had this experience while I was going through a period of great personal trial helped me trust that the Lord could bring a good purpose out of great difficulty. It especially helped me to know that my earthly experience was not just a random collection of events but that God approved my coming to earth at this time to this family and this set of circumstances. My aunt was blessed with visionary gifts that greatly blessed my life.

Our mortal mission will probably include things we premortally wanted to learn and things we wanted to contribute, both as part of a family and individually. We discover them through tackling a variety of learning experiences, seeking the influence of the Holy Ghost, studying our patriarchal blessing, and cooperating with others whose missions and keys intersect with ours. Our missions may include particular family relationships and roles, influence in the lives of specific people or groups, fields of work or study, Church callings or Church service, individual talents and interests, world problems to address, and the development of our character. Both what we choose and what is thrust upon us can help us fulfill our mission, as can both our strengths and our weaknesses, our successes and our failures. When our individual mission includes priesthood purposes, we are entitled to priesthood power to fulfill it.

President Joseph F. Smith saw and named many great prophets and other noble and great leaders, including women, chosen premortally as rulers in God's Church: "Even before they were born, they, with many others, received their first lessons in the world of spirits and were prepared to come forth in the due time of the Lord to labor in his vineyard for the salvation of the souls of men. . . .[10] Among the great and mighty ones who were assembled in this vast congregation of the righteous were Father Adam, the Ancient of Days and father of all, And our glorious Mother Eve, with many of her faithful daughters who had lived through the ages and worshiped the true and living God" (D&C 138:56; 38–39).

In one way or another, our mortal mission will always include serving others. When our daughter Monika was single, she noticed with some frustration that her married friends, especially those with children, were treated like responsible grown-ups in ways she was not. She was in graduate school, owned a home, paid her bills, voted, and got herself to the dentist, but it seemed as though others still thought of her more as a teenager than as an adult. She came to an interesting conclusion: you aren't really seen as an adult until you are helping to raise the next generation.

Monika decided to qualify to do foster care. I frankly thought she'd lost her mind. Taking on children who've been neglected, endangered, or traumatized when you're a single person in graduate school? Bad idea! But Monika, being the adult that she was, ignored me. She made a significant difference in the lives of the children she cared for and came to love. And they made a significant difference in her. Now married with two young children, her husband a doctor and she a university professor, they have been fostering again. I still think they're crazy to take on so much. And noble. And great.

Monika's insight became something of our family's mantra: adults help raise the next generation. We've realized that the "next generation" comes in many forms. My older daughter, also single at that time, decided to help two young women in her ward whose parents had not attended college to explore that option. She took

---

10. See Abraham 3:22.

them to visit a local college campus, helped them get financial aid, got them registered for classes, and followed up to make sure this "next generation" of college students got a good start. My son and his wife started driving new converts in their South Carolina ward to church, taking two cars to accommodate both their own growing family and the "next generation" of members of the Church. My husband and I give financial and emotional support to the "next generations" of missionaries and young adults, also serving on committees and boards that oversee services for them and mentoring them one-on-one.

There are countless ways we can bring new life to this world and help empower the rising generations. This is especially the work of women and men empowered in the name of Christ in the house of the Lord. We do not have to hold a priesthood office to obtain priesthood power to bring people into the circle of our influence, our family, or the family of God.

RAISING THE NEXT GENERATION SPIRITUALLY

It is especially crucial that people with spiritual power help the rising generations toward spiritual rebirth and spiritual growth. Drawing on the experience of a mortal woman giving birth, the scriptures describe a spiritual process of being born again into the kingdom of heaven: "Inasmuch as ye were born into the world by water, and blood, and the spirit, which I have made, and so became of dust a living soul, even so ye must be born again into the kingdom of heaven, of water, and of the Spirit, and be cleansed by blood, even the blood of mine Only Begotten; that ye might be sanctified from all sin, and enjoy the words of eternal life in this world, and eternal life in the world to come, even immortal glory" (Moses 6:59).

Christ takes on the symbolic role of a woman, a mother, in describing His role in our spiritual rebirth. But what does it really mean to be born again? This is the question Nicodemus asked (see John 3:1–17). He knew it couldn't mean going back into our mother's womb and being physically rebirthed, but we sometimes wonder: can we really change who we are without going back in time to get the parents we "deserved" and didn't have, or the life experiences of the rich and famous, or the wisdom to avoid certain problems, or a different body that would have been healthy and whole all along? These are the new births we often hope for, the ones we think would set us free.

I read many years ago, "Forgiveness means giving up hope for a better past."[11] Even though this stark sentence pushes me to accept that of course we have absolutely no hope or possibility of having a better past, it also makes me realize how commonly I wish for exactly that. I'm all for starting over, skipping the setbacks, broken relationships, sicknesses, failings, and mortal weaknesses that feel so limiting and yet so defining. I'm less sure how to work with these barbells life has handed me to build the spiritual muscle they can foster.

I imagine Christ saying in essence to Nicodemus, and to us, "No, indeed, you cannot go back and start over. I'm talking about a different kind of rebirth. One that is possible. And absolutely enough." What does the Atonement of Christ offer us that makes that rebirth possible? He gives us the possibility of looking back on everything in our lives *just exactly as it has been* but through the lens of Christ's power to redeem. Our rebirth does not come from starting over, but from starting a new story about what it all has meant and can mean. This is a story told through the perspective of growth and learning, trusting in the Lord to cash in all our life experience for good if we will let Him. As they did for Joseph Smith, "all these things shall give [us] experience, and shall be for

---

11. Ascribed to Lily Tomlin and various others.

[our] good [because] the Son of Man hath descended below them all" (D&C 122:7–8). This is where true hope lies.

God has given us agency, freedom to choose and to err. But only through the Atonement of Jesus Christ are we truly "free forever"—free to change, free to learn, free to try again without being eternally fettered to the past (2 Nephi 2:26). The Atonement of Christ gives us a rebirth that doesn't come through starting over but through *giving precedence to spiritual realities over physical ones as the genesis of our lives.* The spiritual reality is that our experiences here are not the end of the story, no matter how defining they feel. When we cling to the false hope of turning back the clock as the only thing that could really save us, we refuse the Savior's gift that brings our story to completion or wholeness rather than replacing it.

Our mortal birth to mortal parents is only one part of our story. Christ is birthing the whole. He helps us create a new story about our old life, and a new life out of our old story, and we can do the same for others. When we tell family stories of resilience, strength, and courage, we help create redemption stories for the next generation. When we stop the sins of parents from being passed to children, we help create redemption stories. When we apologize or forgive with a generous heart, we help create redemption stories. When we repent (which means to *change our minds*) of seeing God as one who is shaking His finger at us and instead choose to see Him as one who is beckoning us with love, always on our side, we help create redemption stories.

RAISING THE NEXT GENERATION PHYSICALLY

The priesthood cannot accomplish its purposes without the greatest power God extends to women and men—the power to create, seal, and perpetuate families. President Dallin H. Oaks has taught (quoting President J. Reuben Clark): "The greatest power God has given to His sons cannot be exercised without the companionship of one of His daughters, because only to His daughters has God given the power 'to be a creator of bodies . . . so that God's design and the Great Plan might meet fruition. . . .

"'This is the place of our wives and of our mothers in the Eternal Plan. They are not bearers of the Priesthood; they are not charged with carrying out the duties and functions of the Priesthood; nor are they laden with its responsibilities; they are builders and organizers under its power, and partakers of its blessings, possessing the complement of the Priesthood powers and possessing a function as divinely called, as eternally important in its place as the Priesthood itself.'"[12]

A *complement* is what brings something to completion or perfection. Covenant women in their individual missions as mothers, sisters, leaders, missionaries, teachers, etc. possess "the complement of the Priesthood powers," a complement that brings priesthood authority and power to *completion or perfection.* Parenthood in particular, then, apparently brings to *completion or perfection* the creative, redemptive, governing, priesthood power God bestows in eternity upon sons and daughters who qualify. While priesthood and fatherhood are given to men and sisterhood and motherhood are comparable gifts to women,[13] President M. Russell Ballard makes clear that, "In the eternal perspective, both the procreative power and the priesthood power are shared by husband and wife."[14] This is true even if they do not have offspring.

Jesus Christ has much to teach us about parenthood. We refer to both Jesus Christ and Elohim as Father. Curiously, Isaiah also compares God's relationship to Israel with the relationship of a *mother* and child: "But Zion said, The Lord hath forsaken me,

---

12. Dallin H. Oaks, "The Keys and Authority of the Priesthood," *Ensign*, May 2014, quoting J. Reuben Clark, "Our Wives and Our Mothers in the Eternal Plan," *Relief Society Magazine*, December 1946, 800–801.
13. Spencer W. Kimball, "The Role of Righteous Women," *Ensign*, November 1979.
14. M. Russell Ballard, "This Is My Work and Glory," *Ensign*, May 2013, 19.

and my Lord hath forgotten me. Can a woman forget her sucking child, that she should not have compassion on the son of her womb? yea, they may forget, yet will I not forget thee" (Isaiah 49:14–15).

And later: "As one whom his mother comforteth, so will I comfort you; and ye shall be comforted in Jerusalem" (Isaiah 66:13).

King Benjamin's words about our spiritual rebirth state that Christ both begets (or fathers) us and that we are born of Him: "And now, because of the covenant which ye have made ye shall be called the children of Christ, his sons, and his daughters; for behold, this day he hath spiritually begotten you; for ye say that your hearts are changed through faith on his name; therefore, ye are born of him and have become his sons and his daughters" (Mosiah 5:7).

To summarize, our spiritual "rebirth" as children of Christ draws on the real experience of our mothers conceiving, bearing, laboring, delivering, and feeding us. These experiences included sacrificing body, comfort, and well-being in order to give a body, comfort, and well-being to us. Such experiences speak powerfully to the Savior's sacrifice of body, comfort, and well-being in order to bring new birth to us. It comforts me to see the many ways Jesus Christ was *fruitful*. He shows us by personal example many ways to parent the next generation, whether or not we have children in this life.[15]

We too have many ways to be fruitful in raising the next generation physically. Adoptive parents, foster parents, couples facing infertility, individuals who never marry, and parents who grieve over children they have lost can all resonate with the Savior's role as our adoptive Parent who mourns over lost and missing children.[16] Just as fathers and mothers share "a sacred duty to rear their children in love and righteousness, to provide for their physical and spiritual

---

15. See Mosiah 15:11–13; 2 Peter 1:3–8. See also Ardeth G. Kapp, "Just the Two of Us," *Ensign*, February 1989; and "Faith and Infertility," https://www.lds.org/ensign/2011/04/faith-and-infertility-expanded?lang=eng.
16. See, for example, Jeremiah 31:9; Psalm 68:5; Moses 7:33; 3 Nephi 22:1, 3–5.

needs,"[17] Christ took these roles seriously during His mortal ministry, laboring to provide, comfort, nurture, teach, and love His "seed" (see Mosiah 15:10–11). Christ did not give His followers the more traditional paternal inheritance of land, money, political influence, or status, however. He offered them instead the more maternal gifts of food, healing, teaching, hope, mercy, rebirth, and compassion.

PARTICIPATING IN THE SEALING POWER

Although the priesthood keys of resurrection and creating worlds have not yet been given to mortals,[18] the priesthood authority to create eternal families has.[19] When men and women enter

---

17. "The Family: A Proclamation to the World," *Ensign*, November 2010, 129.
18. See Boyd K. Packer, "Priesthood Power in the Home" (worldwide leadership training meeting, February 2012), lds.org/broadcasts; see also James E. Faust, "Power of the Priesthood," *Ensign*, May 1997, 41–43; Dallin H. Oaks, "The Keys and Authority of the Priesthood," *Ensign*, May 2014.
19. President J. Reuben Clark Jr., "Our Wives and Our Mothers in the Eternal Plan," *Relief Society Magazine*, December 1946, 800–801: "Adam, still in communion with the Father, not yet forgetting that in Heaven parents are not single and that he had a mother there, and still recalling (as we have just pointed out) the Great Plan presented to the Council of Heaven which provided that all the intelligences there assembled were to have the chance to come to earth, receive bodies, and, desiring it, 'keep their second estate,' (Abraham 3:25). Adam, with all this in mind, must have realized the great responsibility which rested upon him; he must have known the part he was to play (for, we must remember, not yet was he shut out from the Father), and he knew, what later, after the Fall, Eve was to sing, (Moses 5:11) that 'he must have seed, that he must know good from evil, that he might have the joy of redemption, and the eternal life which God giveth unto all the obedient.' Adam alone, no matter what his Priesthood, could not bring this about. . . .

    "So came Eve, an helpmeet to the Priesthood mission of Adam—Eve the last created being in the creation of the world, without whom the whole creation of the world would have been in vain and the purposes of God have come to naught. Receiving her, Adam took her in her purity, took her, radiant and divinely fair, into the Garden he had dressed and kept for her, into the bridal home he had built, into the Garden that from then till now has been the symbol of heaven on earth, there to begin together their earthly life, that was finally to bring opportunity for salvation and exaltation to the untold myriads of spirits then waiting for the mortal tabernacles these two were to make it possible for them to possess.

    "The Only Begotten had fashioned the world, had filled it with beautiful flowers and lofty forests, with grasses and grains, and multitudes of living creatures; Adam had had some part in this. But the key to the glorious arch of temporal, earthly creation for man was still missing. So Eve came to build, to organize, through the

the Order of the Son of God through temple covenants, including the holy order of matrimony in the new and everlasting covenant, they obtain priesthood authority and power to organize and administer an eternal family in this life or the next.[20] As explored in the beautiful children's book *Our Heavenly Family, Our Earthly Families*, our life here can resemble our heavenly home, and we can be assured that we have a Mother in Heaven as on earth.[21]

Women throughout the world give birth, but women who have been sealed in the temple to a spouse give birth to children who are "born in the covenant." These children are born as legal heirs to all the priesthood blessings, privileges, and responsibilities of that covenant, contingent on being personally vested with those priestly identities in the temple as adults. A woman giving birth "in the covenant" bestows a "birthright" on that child that is both essential and otherwise attainable only through the sealing power of the priesthood. In this sense, covenant women married in the temple have a type of sealing power. We usually think of ordinances as symbolic representations of mighty spiritual realities we need to attain, but in this case, it looks more like the sealing ordinance is the symbol and birth in the covenant is itself one of the "mighty realities."

When children not born in the covenant are sealed to parents, then, they not only gain the assurance of eternal association with those parents, but they become lawful heirs to a priesthood birthright, just like children born in the covenant. Elder Theodore M. Burton explains: "One thing we often fail to realize is that our priesthood comes to us through the lineage of our fathers and mothers. The Lord explained it in these words: 'Therefore, thus

---

power of the Father, the bodies of mortal men, to be a creator of bodies under the faculties given her by the Priesthood of God, so that God's design and the Great Plan might meet fruition."

20. See Ezra Taft Benson, "What I Hope You Will Teach Your Children about the Temple," *Temples of the Church of Jesus Christ of Latter-day Saints* (1988), 42–45.
21. McArthur Krishna and Bethany Brady Spalding, *Our Heavenly Family, Our Earthly Families* (Salt Lake City: Deseret Book, 2016).

saith the Lord unto you, with whom the priesthood hath continued through the lineage of your fathers. . . .' (D&C 86:8).

"'Oh,' I can hear some of you say, 'there must be something wrong with that statement, for I am the only member of my family who has joined the Church. How could I have received the priesthood from my parents?'

"In this scripture the Lord was not talking about your priesthood line of authority. He was talking about your inherited right to receive and use priesthood power. . . .

"The Lord continues the revelation: 'For ye are lawful heirs, according to the flesh, and have been hid from the world with Christ in God' (D&C 86:9)."[22]

Children become "lawful heirs" of the "right to receive and use priesthood power" either by being born into the covenant or being sealed to covenant parents later in life or by proxy after they die. Thus mothers and fathers authoritatively participate in the priesthood power of "bind[ing] on earth what shall be bound in heaven" (D&C 128:8), acting "in the earth for the salvation of the human family," in the words of President Joseph F. Smith's definition of priesthood, quoted previously.[23] Regarding this eternal order, recall Brigham Young's conversation with Joseph Smith after Joseph's death, in which Joseph taught him, "Our Father in heaven organized the human family, but they are all disorganized and in great confusion." Joseph also taught Brigham that if the Latter-day Saints keep the Spirit, "They will find themselves just as they were organized by our Father in Heaven before they came into the world."[24]

Just as not all men of covenant hold the priesthood, become

---

22. Theodore M. Burton, "Salvation for the Dead—a Missionary Activity," *Ensign*, May 1975.
23. Joseph Fielding Smith, ed., *Gospel Doctrine: Selections from the Sermons and Writings of Joseph F. Smith*, 5th ed. (Salt Lake City: Deseret Book, 1939), 139.
24. Brigham Young, from Elden J. Watson, ed., *Manuscript History of Brigham Young, 1846–1847* (Salt Lake City: Elden J. Watson), 528–30.

fathers, or are temple sealers or patriarchs, not all covenant women marry or bear children and not all children are born in the covenant. Nevertheless, in the mercy and grace of the Lord, all are offered the opportunity for eternal relationships. In one sense, the purpose of the Church is to make sure all of the blessings available to any of God's children are available to each one of His children. Specifically, sealing children to parents ensures each child will receive a full and eternal spiritual birthright within the family of God. Equally important to the words of the sealer is the physical, priestly presence of the man and woman who kneel at the altar to create a priesthood and familial context for each child to be sealed into. Likewise, all the currently barren "mothers and fathers" in Israel will one day have eternal offspring, for this is our identity and birthright. For now, we are to mourn together, comfort one another, and withhold all judgment when some of us must wait.

Perhaps such waiting can strengthen our compassion for the majority of God's children, who will have to wait for the next life and the kindness of someone else to make the blessings of eternal family available to them and their children vicariously. Blessedly, adoptive parents, new converts, and those who are not endowed or sealed until after their children are born can obtain and offer their children these blessings in this life, and children who did not inherit these rights at birth can attain them through a temple sealing. Adoptive parents' redemptive roles in the lives of their children can more than make up for the often less than ideal circumstances into which they were born. Adoption allows parents to participate in God's holy work of overcoming every limitation of mortality to which we are all subject. Adoption is a symbol of a mighty reality: we are all adopted into the family of Christ when we become truly converted and are baptized.

Your personal contribution to our collective human understanding of God's love may come through your experience with loving your own children, or with loving someone else's children, or with longing to have children to love, or with the impact on your soul of indifference or distortions of love. But if we are truly all in this together, and we are, then each of these contributions, though potentially challenging, is also potentially Zion-building and life-giving.

PATRIARCH, ANOTHER WORD FOR PARENT

We often refer to ancient prophets as patriarchs, but in the broadest sense, patriarchs are fathers. Patriarchs (fathers in the ancient world) passed on their land, records, power, and priesthood rights to their posterity.[25] If your own father didn't have these things, or if you were not the oldest or favored son, your birthright was limited by these artifacts. Today, all of God's worthy and desiring children can be heirs to the promises made to the patriarchs of old, promises disseminated (interesting word) across the world and across time. We can live up to our privilege of participating in the work of organizing the family of God as perfectly as we can through family history work and completing temple ordinances. We can all help all the youth of the Church aspire to be vested in the temple and priesthood blessings they are entitled to. We can order our own lives and families after the example of our spiritual Father, Jesus Christ. And we can participate in the parental role of patriarchs as either physical or spiritual fathers or mothers in our own relationships.

Priesthood operates in the Church at large to ensure doctrinal purity and good governance, but fathers and mothers still preside over and govern within their families. The Aaronic Priesthood in ancient days was held by only Aaron and his unblemished sons properly vested with that authority, but Jewish fathers and mothers

---

25. See, for example, Abraham 1:2–4, 18–19, 31; 2:19; Genesis 22:17.

bless their children at home using words and forms that would otherwise be reserved for priests (see Numbers 6:22–27).

President Oaks reminds us: "The authority that presides in the family—whether father or single-parent mother—functions in family matters without the need to get authorization from anyone holding priesthood keys. This family authority includes directing the activities of the family, family meetings like family home evenings, family prayer, teaching the gospel, and counseling and disciplining family members."[26]

TEMPLE PRIVILEGES

I read about world leaders abusing power, or drug cartels in Utah, or wars displacing millions, and it is almost amazing to me that I can drive to the grocery store without bodyguards. It can feel as if the world is a powder keg waiting to blow. These disturbing realities make the warnings of scripture about the last days feel all too real.

I also know it is crucial not to "take counsel from [my] fears," but to remember with gratitude every good and peaceful day I've lived and to reflect on the regenerating promises to this rising generation: "And it shall come to pass in the last days, saith God, I will pour out of my Spirit upon all flesh: and your sons and your daughters shall prophesy, and your young men shall see visions, and your old men shall dream dreams: And on my servants and on my handmaidens I will pour out in those days of my Spirit; and they shall prophesy" (Acts 2:17–18).

"Thus saith the Lord that made thee, and formed thee from the womb, which will help thee; Fear not, O Jacob, my servant. . . . For I will pour water upon him that is thirsty, and floods upon the

---

26. Dallin H. Oaks, "Priesthood Authority in the Family and the Church," *Ensign*, November 2005.

dry ground: I will pour my spirit upon thy seed, and my blessing upon thine offspring" (Isaiah 44:2–3).

The temple can be a refuge of peace, a school in revelatory power, a birthing room of the soul. President Boyd K. Packer taught: "No work is more of a protection to this church than temple work and the genealogical research that supports it. No work is more spiritually refining. No work we do gives us more power. Our labors in the temple cover us with a shield and a protection, both individually and as a people."[27]

The rights of patriarchs and sealers can gloriously expand to parents and covenant adults as we develop the visionary gifts of the Spirit, fulfill our personal missions, facilitate the spiritual and physical rebirth of the rising generation, seal families both across time and in place, and empower others to do likewise.

---

27. Boyd K. Packer, "The Holy Temple," *Ensign*, February 1995.

Chapter 10
WITNESS
SEVENTY, APOSTLE

And with great power gave the apostles witness of the resurrection of the Lord Jesus: and great grace was upon them all.

ACTS 4:33

It is an incredible privilege, shared by only a tiny fraction of all who have inhabited this planet, to have living witnesses of the Resurrection of the Savior Jesus Christ in our midst. In addition to being crucial to Church governance, the offices of Seventy and Apostle remind us that God wants to be known to His people. He can be sought, and He can be found by each of us.

SPECIAL WITNESSES: SEVENTIES

Both Apostles and Seventies are called as special witnesses of Jesus Christ in all the world. General Authorities in Christ's Church hold unique keys. It is their responsibility to guide His Church under the influence and approval of His Spirit.

Let's consider first the office of Seventy, which seems to have originated with the Lord inviting Moses to bring seventy of the leaders and officers in Israel to the "tabernacle of the congregation"

> **DUTIES OF THE OFFICE OF SEVENTY**
>
> - "Preach the gospel, and . . . be especial witnesses unto the Gentiles and in all the world" (D&C 107:25)
> - "Act in the name of the Lord, under the direction of the Twelve . . . in building up the church and regulating all the affairs of the same in all nations" (v. 34)
> - "Be traveling ministers" (v. 97)

(Numbers 11:16). This phrase has also been translated as the "tent of meeting" because it was not like a stake center for simply "congregating" but a place outside the camp of daily life for a much more personal encounter with God. It was God's residence on earth—a temple.

These seventy leaders were called to stand with Moses in bearing the burden of leadership in the house of Israel (see Numbers 11:16–17). They were invited to stand around the "tent of meeting" where God would come to strengthen them, speaking to them from a great cloud (see v. 25). There the seventy were filled with the spirit of prophecy.

Curiously, two leaders who had not gone with the seventy to the tabernacle were equally filled with the spirit of prophecy "in the camp." This serves as a quiet reminder to me that God is not tucked away in a place unreachable to me. He can come into my ordinary life: "For the Lord thy God walketh in the midst of thy camp" (Deuteronomy 23:14). However, Joshua, the future leader of Israel, concerned about the propriety of these men prophesying "in the camp," brought it to Moses's attention: "And Moses said unto him, Enviest thou for my sake? would God that all the Lord's people were prophets, and that the Lord would put his spirit upon them!" (Numbers 11:29).

Moses, the prophet who had seen God face to face, yearned to see his privileges and the privileges of the seventy given to all the children of Israel: "Now this Moses plainly taught to the children of Israel in the wilderness, and sought diligently to sanctify his people that they might behold the face of God; But they hardened their hearts and could not endure his presence; therefore, the Lord in his wrath, for his anger was kindled against them, swore that they should not enter into his rest while in the wilderness, which rest is the fulness of his glory. Therefore, he took Moses out of their midst, and the Holy Priesthood also" (D&C 84:23–25).

In our dispensation, those holding the office of Seventy also help bear the burden of leadership of the Church and are called to "preach the gospel, and to be especial witnesses [of the name of Christ] . . . in all the world" (D&C 107:25). And today, as in times past, it is still the hope of prophets and of the Lord that people "in the camp" will also be filled with God's Spirit.

> ### DUTIES OF THE OFFICE OF APOSTLE
>
> - Be "special witnesses of the name of Christ in all the world" (D&C 107:23)
> - "Hold the keys to open up the authority of [Christ's] kingdom upon the four corners of the earth" (D&C 124:128)
> - Preach faith in Christ, repentance, baptism, and the gift of the Holy Ghost "to every creature" (D&C 49:11–14)
> - "Prune my vineyard for the last time, . . . that I may pour out my Spirit upon all flesh" (D&C 95:4)

SPECIAL WITNESSES OF CHRIST: APOSTLES

Apostles have been called both anciently and in our day as "special witness[es][1] of the name of Jesus Christ in all the world,

---

1. Elder Ronald A. Rasband asked President Boyd K. Packer about language in the Doctrine and Covenants that describes the role of the Twelve as "special witnesses" (D&C 107:23) and the role of the Seventy as "especial witnesses" (D&C 107:25). There is no subtle difference between the two, President Packer said. "The difference between *especial* and *special* is in the spelling, and it really does not mean anything more than that. To be a special witness of the name of Christ means that you have that witness and that authority that is unfailing, and it will be with you everywhere in the world." https://www.lds.org/prophets-and-apostles/unto-all-the-world/the-twelve-and-the-seventy-part-three-witnesses-to-the-world?lang=eng.

particularly of His divinity and of His bodily resurrection from the dead" (Bible Dictionary; see also D&C 107:23–24; Acts 4:33). A type of apostolic office was also established in the Book of Mormon (see 3 Nephi 12:1; 13:25). Jesus Christ, the messenger of the covenant, is also called an Apostle (see Hebrews 3:1), reminding us that He functions in all the duties and privileges of His priesthood.

The word *apostle* means something like "one sent forth" (Bible Dictionary, "Apostle"). The Bible Dictionary also notes that some of those referred to as apostles may not have formally served in the Twelve. As eyewitnesses of Christ's Resurrection and divinity, they were still apostles "strictly in the sense of being special witnesses for the Lord Jesus Christ." President Russell M. Nelson teaches: "Apostolic just means 'one called away.' . . . You don't have to be an ordained Apostle with a capital A to be one of His disciples. If you're 'carried away' in the work of the Lord you're by definition an apostle."[2]

The First Presidency and the Twelve carry the primary responsibility of leading the covenant people of God according to His will. This responsibility is heavy, and Jesus Christ promises to strengthen them with His Spirit, His angels, and His presence: "And as I said unto mine apostles, even so I say unto you, for you are mine apostles, even God's high priests; ye are they whom my Father hath given me; ye are my friends. . . . And whoso receiveth you, there I will be also, for I will go before your face. I will be on your right hand and on your left, and my Spirit shall be in your hearts, and mine angels round about you, to bear you up" (D&C 84:63, 88).

The lofty promises in this last verse are also addressed "unto all the faithful who are called of God in the church unto the ministry" (D&C 84:86). The Lord in fact promises that "every soul" who

---

2. BYU Jerusalem Center address, April 8, 2018, https://www.lds.org/broadcasts/watch/special-jerusalem-broadcast/2018/04?lang=eng.

qualifies may, in the spirit of the offices of Seventy and Apostle, gain a personal witness of the Resurrection and divinity of Jesus Christ: "Verily, thus saith the Lord: It shall come to pass that every soul who forsaketh his sins and cometh unto me, and calleth on my name, and obeyeth my voice, and keepeth my commandments, shall see my face and know that I am" (D&C 93:1; see also Exodus 19:11; Matthew 5:8; 2 Nephi 11:3; Ether 4:7, among others).

The process of aligning our personal identity with that of the Savior is described by President Dallin H. Oaks as he explores the meaning of the word *willing* in the sacrament prayer: "We may think of the sacramental covenant to take upon us the name of Jesus Christ as comprising at least three meanings, each expressive of . . . [an] ascending level of spiritual progress or maturity. First, we signify our willingness to be identified as a believer in Jesus Christ and as a member of the Church that bears His name. . . . Second, we signify our willingness to take upon us our assigned measure of the authority and work of the Savior to bring to pass the eternal life of the children of God, including accepting and laboring diligently to fulfill the responsibilities of our own callings in His kingdom. Third, we witness our commitment to strive for exaltation in the celestial kingdom."[3]

He describes this last level of spiritual progress or maturity as follows: "This meaning of taking His name upon us concerns our relationship to our Savior and the incomprehensible blessings available to those who will eventually achieve what the Apostle Paul called 'a perfect man [or woman],[4] unto the measure of the stature of the fulness of Christ:' (Eph. 4:13). . . . In this sacred sense, our witness that we are 'willing to take upon us the name of Jesus Christ' constitutes our declaration of candidacy for exaltation. . . .

---

3. Dallin H. Oaks, *His Holy Name* (Salt Lake City: Deseret Book, 2009).
4. Oaks, *His Holy Name*; brackets in original.

[and] our determination to do all that we can to come unto Christ and receive the fulness of the Father."

President Oaks clarifies, "Only upon His action will we actually take His holy name upon us in this important sense."[5]

The Melchizedek Priesthood, extant among the Book of Mormon and New Testament Churches (see Alma 13:1–6; Luke 10:1), has been restored in our day—priesthood with the authority, ordinances, power, and promises to bring us into God's presence. Apostles and Seventies are charged with obtaining, and sharing with the world, personal witnesses of God's presence among His people. Nevertheless, each of us can either obtain for ourselves, through study, pondering, prayer, and the witness of the Holy Ghost, a testimony of the divinity, Resurrection, and saving power of Jesus Christ, or we can be blessed with the ability to believe the testimonies of those who have. If we continue faithful, those in either group are heirs of eternal life (see D&C 46:13–14). Joseph Smith has further promised: "God hath not revealed anything to Joseph, but what He will make known unto the Twelve, and even the least Saint may know all things as fast as he is able to bear them; for the day must come when no man need say to his neighbor, Know ye the Lord; for all shall know Him . . . from the least to the greatest [see Jeremiah 31:34]."[6]

WOMEN AS WITNESSES OF CHRIST

I am especially grateful that women are among those whose personal witnesses of Jesus's divinity and Resurrection are recorded in scripture. In fact, the first mortal to receive a personal witness of the divinity of the Holy Child Jesus was His mother, Mary (see Luke 1:35). The first mortal to receive a personal witness of

---

5. Oaks, *His Holy Name*.
6. *Teachings of Presidents of the Church: Joseph Smith* (Salt Lake City: The Church of Jesus Christ of Latter-day Saints, 2007).

the Resurrection of Jesus Christ was Mary Magdalene (see John 20:14–17). The first account we have of Jesus specifically declaring Himself as the Messiah was to the Samaritan woman at the well who so needed His saving power (see John 4:25–26).

Women in the Book of Mormon also received personal witnesses of the Savior. The wife of the Lamanite king Lamoni was overcome by the Spirit along with her husband, their servants, and the missionary Ammon. The queen was raised from this state by the touch and faith of her handmaid, Abish, a convert to Christ of many years. The queen then raised the king. He described seeing his Redeemer, and then she too describes, "O blessed Jesus, who has saved me from an awful hell! O blessed God, have mercy on this people!" (Alma 19:29). The resurrected Savior also appeared in a most personal way to women in the Book of Mormon, along with men (beyond the twelve disciples called to lead) and children: "And the multitude did see and hear and bear record; and they know that their record is true for they all of them did see and hear, every man for himself; and they were in number about two thousand and five hundred souls; and they did consist of men, women, and children" (3 Nephi 17:25).

IS DISCIPLESHIP WORTH IT?

It doesn't take long as we seek to follow the Savior, however, before it dawns on us that the path He trod led to Gethsemane and Golgotha. These are places we simply do not want to go, not ever. We read of God weeping over His children (see Moses 7:28, 32–33), we contemplate the evil in this world, we experience our own heartbreaks and betrayals, we see Christ's ultimate sacrifice, and we can wonder most sincerely why anyone would want to "be like Jesus." Christ's Atonement does so much for us, but did it do anything for Him? Or did it only cost Him? We may suddenly see His life as having "no form nor comeliness; and when we shall see him, there is no beauty that we should desire him [because] He is despised and rejected of men; a man of sorrows, and acquainted with grief" (Isaiah 53:2–3). Can exaltation possibly be worth the perils and pain of such a journey?

There has to be more to qualifying for exaltation than white-knuckling sorrow, like getting tenure in a job we wouldn't want anyway. Maybe the blessing of seeing God's face would not just be assurance that He approves of our life and that we are enough. Maybe the blessing of seeing God's face, even in small moments of life "in the camp," would be to see that He approves of *His* life, because His life is full of *life*—of joy, meaning, peace, creativity, redemption, and sweetness, pressed down and running over.

The Savior's fullness of sorrow and suffering was truly experienced in the Old World. But the Book of Mormon shows us the rest of the story: the fullness of His joy. Those who witnessed this joy both shared in it and testified of it: "And after this manner do they bear record: The eye hath never seen, neither hath the ear heard, before, so great and marvelous things as we saw and heard Jesus speak unto the Father; And no tongue can speak, neither can there be written by any man, neither can the hearts of men conceive so great and marvelous things as we both saw and heard Jesus speak; and *no one can conceive of the joy which filled our souls* at the time we heard him pray for us unto the Father. And it came to pass that when Jesus had made an end of praying unto the Father, he arose; but *so great was the joy of the multitude that they were overcome*. And it came to pass that Jesus spake unto them, and bade them arise. And they arose from the earth, and he said unto them: Blessed are ye because of your faith. And now behold, *my joy is full*" (3 Nephi 17:16–20; emphasis added).

Even death loses its sting and terror as the reality of what awaits us in eternity becomes sure. But we can also truly triumph *now* over foes of sin, loss, and fear, superseding them with an assurance of *life* that breaks through eternity and into time. Even with the relentlessness of death pressing down day by day, as it does upon us all, we can also live "in newness of life" day by day (Romans 6:4).

EARNEST MONEY ON THE TREASURES OF ETERNITY

When people offer to buy a house, they generally include "earnest money" with the offer—a deposit to show the buyer they are serious about following through if all the terms of the purchase agreement are met. The Lord also gives us "earnest" on His covenants: "Now he which stablisheth us with you in Christ, and hath anointed us, is God; Who hath also sealed us, and given the *earnest* of the Spirit in our hearts" (2 Corinthians 1:21–22; emphasis added).

The word translated here as *earnest* is elsewhere translated as *deposit*, *pledge*, or *guarantee*. For example, another Bible translation reads: "Now it is God who makes both us and you stand firm in Christ. He anointed us, set his seal of ownership on us, and put his Spirit in our hearts as a deposit, guaranteeing what is to come."[7]

The gift of the Holy Ghost—the "Spirit in our hearts"—is God's "earnest money" to us on the promises of eternity. These gifts give us hope, help us endure to the end, and tutor us in spiritual power. The first Comforter not only prepares us for the Second Comforter but also helps us live in newness of life today.

There are countless examples of prophets, General Authorities, and holy men in scripture exercising miracles and spiritual gifts. Here is a tiny smattering of examples of ordinary women doing so:

The gifts of prophecy and miracles (see D&C 46:21–22). About a year after being called as an Apostle, Elder Dale G. Renlund was traveling with Elder Hugo Martinez, a Seventy, in South America to Georgetown, Guyana, for a district conference.

---

7. 2 Corinthians 1:21–22, New International Version of the Bible.

As they rushed to get in line for their connection in Panama City, a woman who was also preparing to board the plane approached them and asked in Spanish, "Are you members of The Church of Jesus Christ of Latter-day Saints?" Remember, Apostles and Seventies don't wear name tags like missionaries do, nor was this woman even a member of the Church. Elder Martinez, who speaks Spanish, told her they were. The story continues:

"'Can you help me?' she asked. She wasn't a member of the Church and needed help with a complicated membership issue relating to a deceased relative.

"'I had served on a committee that dealt with these complicated membership issues in the year and a half before my call to the Twelve,' said Elder Renlund. 'So I knew what information we needed and what we could do to help.' As he reached into his briefcase, pulled out a card and explained to her what she needed to do, she burst into tears. She said, 'I knew you could help me because I saw you last night in a dream.'

"She emailed Elder Renlund, and they resolved the problem. 'Her children, who are members of the Church and are also relatives of this individual, were just so overjoyed to have this resolved,' he said. After the resolution, Monica wrote Elder Renlund and said, 'My children now believe in miracles.'"[8]

This story touches me deeply, not just because Elder Renlund as an Apostle was in the right place at the right time with the right experience to help, but because a faithful woman, not a member of the Church and yet faithfully engaged in the work of saving the human family, elicited this miracle.

The gift of knowledge (see D&C 46:18). In the 1880s, women were encouraged to gain education in medicine and health care to

---

8. Sarah Jane Weaver, "Inside the Quorum of the Twelve: What It's Like to Be a Prophet, Seer, and Revelator," *Church News*, June 17, 2018, https://www.lds.org/church/news/inside-the-quorum-of-the-twelve-what-its-like-to-be-a-prophet-seer-and-revelator?cid=HP_SA-21-7-2018_dPTH_fCNWS_xLIDyL1-C_&lang=eng.

serve as midwives in Utah. The mother of future Church President Joseph Fielding Smith, Julina L. Smith, "followed this counsel and received training to serve as a midwife. She often awoke him in the middle of the night so he could drive their horse-drawn carriage to a home where a baby was about to be born. Serving with his mother in this way, young Joseph Fielding Smith saw an example of the strength and compassion of the women of the Church."[9]

The gift of faith to be healed (see D&C 46:19). The faith of the woman with an issue of blood allowed her to be healed by touching the clothes of Jesus (see Luke 8:43–48).

The gift of faith to heal (see D&C 46:20). Amanda Smith was in the wrong place at the wrong time in 1838 when a mob attacked the Saints at Hawn's Mill in Missouri. Her husband and one son were killed, and another son, Alma, had his hip blown away by a gun blast. In response to her fervent prayer, she felt directed to clean out the wound and pack it with a poultice, seeing in a vision that the Lord would make the boy a new hip. Alma lay still for five weeks until he recovered, a "flexible gristle having grown in place of the missing joint and socket, . . . a marvel to physicians." She writes: "On the day that he walked again I was out of the house fetching a bucket of water, when I heard screams from the children. Running back, in affright, I entered, and there was Alma on the floor, dancing around, and the children screaming in astonishment and joy."[10]

The gift of faith to command the natural world (see Jacob 4:6–7). My friend Bridget went with her family on an elephant ride in Thailand. She and her mother-in-law shared an elephant with a stubborn streak that lagged behind the others, despite the prodding of the guide. The dirt road was cut into the hillside with

---

9. *Teachings of Presidents of the Church: Joseph Fielding Smith* (Salt Lake City: The Church of Jesus Christ of Latter-day Saints, 2013), 297–309.
10. Amanda Barnes Smith, in Edward W. Tullidge, *The Women of Mormondom* (Salt Lake City: lithograph reprint of 1877 original, 1965), 124, 128.

a steep drop-off into the valley below, and at one point the elephant pulled away from the guide and started backing toward the edge. Bridget and her mother-in-law were flung side to side as the guide shouted and prodded, but the elephant dropped one leg precariously off the edge. Bridget writes, "Time slowed way down. If the elephant backed up any further, his legs would buckle and he would roll down the cliff and crush us. I began to pray aloud, 'Heavenly Father, please help us!' Grandma Janet froze, her breathing labored as she struggled to stay erect in her seat. A flash of clarity came into my mind. *If I am living worthy, I have the power to command through the name of Jesus Christ.* I forcefully said, 'In the name of Jesus Christ, I command you, elephant, to walk back to camp.' AND HE DID. He pulled his rear leg back onto the narrow dirt road and walked purposefully back to camp. I cried and shouted for joy and relief. Our prayers were answered. We were protected."[11]

The gifts of speaking in tongues and of interpretation of tongues (see D&C 46:24–25). In 1876, Eliza R. Snow and Zina Young toured Utah organizing the Young Ladies' National Mutual Improvement Association among the wards of the Church. Martha Healey was called as the secretary to this association in Alpine, Utah. The president and her five counselors were all young single women except one counselor, who was seventeen and a newlywed. "The meeting was held at the home of Bishop McCullough. Sister Snow gave each new officer a blessing in 'tongues,' then Sister Young laid her hands on the heads of each officer giving the interpretation and meaning of the tongues. This was the first time these ladies had experienced 'tongues.'"[12]

The gift of preaching (see Alma 9:21). In the late 1880s,

---

11. Personal correspondence.
12. Jennie Adams Wild, *Alpine Yesterdays: A History of Alpine, Utah County, Utah, 1850–1980* (Alpine City, 1982), 96.

Elizabeth McCune, a wealthy Latter-day Saint woman from Utah, traveled to Great Britain with her husband and children on an extended holiday. A book that had recently been published there by a former Latter-day Saint was especially critical of the Church's treatment of women, and the all-male missionaries struggled to refute its claims. Sister McCune was invited on a few hours' notice to speak at the evening session of the Church's London Conference. Word spread, and the hall filled with both members and curious spectators. Elizabeth told the group she had traveled extensively and had never "found women held in such esteem as among the Mormons of Utah." She continued, "Our husbands are proud of their wives and daughters; they do not consider that they were created solely to wash dishes and tend babies; but they give them every opportunity to attend meetings and lectures and to take up everything which will educate and develop them. Our religion teaches us that the wife stands shoulder to shoulder with the husband." She was so effective that she was asked to speak repeatedly. The European Mission presidency soon wrote to the First Presidency asking for capable sister missionaries to be sent. Six months later, the First Presidency decided to call single sister missionaries for the first time in Church history, complete with certificates authorizing them to preach the gospel.[13]

The gift of "exceedingly great" faith (see Moroni 10:11). In 1987, the Pilcomayo River in Paraguay flooded, twice, wiping out homes, farms, livestock, and the chapel of a group of Latter-day Saints living near its banks. They were in knee-deep water for over a month and relocated twice. Eventually, Elder Ted E. Brewerton of the Seventy was dispatched with a rescue party to try to help. He found their situation bleak but their faces peaceful. That evening at the branch meeting a sister offered a prayer Elder Brewerton

---

13. Matthew S. McBride, "I Could Have Gone into Every House," *Women of Conviction* website (2012), https://history.lds.org/article/elizabeth-mccune-missionary?lang=eng.

will always remember. She said, "Father, we have lost our beautiful chapel, we have lost our clothing, we no longer have homes, . . . we don't have any materials to build anything, we have to walk ten kilometers to get a drink of dirty river water and [we] don't have a bucket. But we desire to express to thee our gratitude for our good health, for our happiness, and for our Church membership. Father, we want thee to know that under any conditions, we will be true, strong, and faithful to the covenants we made to thee when we were baptized."[14]

GOD WORKS BY POWER

Moroni pleads: "Deny not the power of God; for he worketh by power, according to the faith of the children of men, the same today and tomorrow, and forever. And again, I exhort you, my brethren [and sisters], that ye deny not the gifts of God, for they are many; and they come from the same God" (Moroni 10:7–8).

As apostles and prophets continue in their unique commission as overseers under Jesus Christ of the "ongoing process" of the Restoration,[15] how grateful I am that the Holy Ghost can be the constant companion of every member of Christ's Church, bringing revelation, miracles, and spiritual power into our lives. Our dominion within the kingdom of God and in the lives of other people can flow unto us peacefully, joyfully, and "without compulsory means . . . forever and ever" (D&C 121:45–46). These blessings are our "earnest," a pledge and deposit on this promise: The privileges offered to apostles and prophets of knowing the Savior Jesus Christ can one day be ours.

---

14. Elaine L. Jack, "Partakers of the Glories," *Ensign*, October 1996 (referencing Heidi S. Swinton, *Pioneer Spirit* [1996], 8–11).
15. Dieter F. Uchtdorf, "Are You Sleeping through the Restoration?" *Ensign*, May 2014.

Conclusion
MORE THAN YESTERDAY, LESS THAN TOMORROW

Now the great and grand secret of the whole matter, and the summum bonum of the whole subject that is lying before us, consists in obtaining the powers of the Holy Priesthood.

DOCTRINE AND COVENANTS 128:11

As a therapist for others and in my own life, I've realized that one of my greatest opportunities for learning and growth is to be stuck in a confining circumstance I cannot change. Ironically, constraints (like the limited options at my small neighborhood grocery store) can sometimes help me not be immobilized by too many choices. Sometimes constraints (like the literary specifications for a sonnet) spur my creativity because I have to think outside the box of the easiest or most obvious choices. And sometimes constraints (like a relationship I cannot easily get out of) push me to expand my skills, question my assumptions, or deepen my commitment to what I value most. At first blush it may seem as though having more options instead of less would always be preferable, but often I more easily focus, I become more creative, I am more motivated to hone my skills, I more readily uncover faulty assumptions, and

I deepen my commitment to my highest values by having to work within constraints or limitations.

When people's options are oppressive, overly confining, or blatantly unfair, I will and must work to expand them. But sometimes the most helpful question I can ask is, "Given what I cannot change, what are my deepest values for how I want to live now?" In other words, sometimes I don't need expanded options as much as I need expanded vision of what is possible within the options I have.

Sister Bonnie L. Oscarson has taught: "All women need to see themselves as essential participants in the work of the priesthood. . . . The kingdom of God cannot function unless we rise up and fulfill our duties with faith. Sometimes we just need to have a greater vision of what is possible."[1]

It is my hope that this book has helped broaden our vision of what is possible. Even more, I hope it has helped us trust that faithful women and men—whether or not we hold power in a worldly sense—can grow in power in the priesthood as we understand the priesthood authority we have been given, clarify and live our deepest values, hone the skill of discerning and acting on the promptings and gifts of the Holy Ghost, and relentlessly grow toward our highest spiritual potential. I have no illusions about this book being a definitive statement about how that all happens; however, I hope it has provided some initial inroads into territory others will continue to explore with courage and to map with precision.

COVENANT PROMISES

Sister Linda K. Burton has taught: "As God commissions women and men to engage in His work of salvation for all of the human family, He gives us all the right and responsibility to

---

1. Bonnie L. Oscarson, "Rise Up in Strength, Sisters in Zion," *Ensign*, November 2016.

obtain and magnify His power and become heirs of His covenant promises."[2]

Which of the covenant promises you've received through baptism, temple covenants, your understanding of the scriptures, your patriarchal blessing or other blessings, or the oath and covenant of the priesthood matter most to you? I will say unabashedly that I want to fulfill my personal mission and make a difference for good for people I love. I want healing and help and the ministering of angels. I want to be a living disciple and witness of Jesus Christ and to organize my life according to His laws. I want my family relationships to be healthy, holy, and enduring. I want to build Zion. I want to live in newness of life each day. I want to know God, trust Him completely with my life, and feel at home in His presence.

These desires are aspects of the promised inheritance of covenant women and men who engage in God's work of saving the human family—His family. Our personal righteousness coupled with the gift and gifts of the Holy Ghost qualify us to ask the Lord to turn these promises into realities. President Lorenzo Snow promises: "This is the grand privilege of every Latter-day Saint . . . that it is our right to have the manifestations of the Spirit every day of our lives."[3]

Oh, what a privilege! But one I absolutely do not live up to. I get distracted. I am busy. I hesitate to feel and name my feelings to God and deal with them according to my deepest values. I worry He'll give me too much to do. I listen to the voice of the accuser instead of the voice of my Advocate, Jesus Christ. Instead of taking courage, I "take counsel from [my] fears."[4] I live below my privileges. I am a long way from home.

But I am on the road.

---

2. Linda K. Burton, "Priesthood Power—Available to All," BYU Women's Conference address, May 2, 2013.
3. *Teachings of Presidents of the Church: Lorenzo Snow* (Salt Lake City: The Church of Jesus Christ of Latter-day Saints, 2012), 76.
4. James E. Faust, "Be Not Afraid," *Ensign,* October 2002.

PRIESTHOOD POWER THROUGH PRIESTHOOD RESPONSIBILITIES

"AND NOW CONTINUE YOUR JOURNEY"[5]

Now what? Now I need help. If you heard President Nelson speak at his first general conference as President of the Church on Easter Sunday, 2018, perhaps you remember his invitation and plea: "What wisdom do you lack? What do you feel an urgent need to know or understand? Follow the example of the Prophet Joseph. Find a quiet place where you can regularly go. Humble yourself before God. Pour out your heart to your Heavenly Father. Turn to Him for answers and for comfort.

"Pray in the name of Jesus Christ about your concerns, your fears, your weaknesses—yes, the very longings of your heart. And then listen! Write the thoughts that come to your mind. Record your feelings and follow through with actions that you are prompted to take. As you repeat this process day after day, month after month, year after year, you will 'grow into the principle of revelation.'[6] . . .

"Our Savior and Redeemer, Jesus Christ, will perform some of His mightiest works between now and when He comes again. . . . But in coming days, it will not be possible to survive spiritually without the guiding, directing, comforting, and constant influence of the Holy Ghost.

"My beloved brothers and sisters, I plead with you to increase your spiritual capacity to receive revelation. Let this Easter Sunday be a defining moment in your life. Choose to do the spiritual work required to enjoy the gift of the Holy Ghost and hear the voice of the Spirit more frequently and more clearly."[7]

Let's review: 1) In a quiet place, we're to pour out our heart to God about our concerns, fears, weaknesses, and longings. 2) We're to write down the thoughts that come to mind. 3) We're to act

---

5. Doctrine and Covenants 62:4.
6. *Teachings: Joseph Smith*, 132, as quoted by President Nelson.
7. Russell M. Nelson, "Revelation for the Church, Revelation for Our Lives," *Ensign*, May 2018.

as prompted. 4) We're to repeat this day after day, month after month, year after year.

But I'll confess: 1) When I sleepily kneel each morning, sometimes I don't have much to say, and sometimes God doesn't seem to either. 2) When I try to write down impressions, sometimes I'm not sure I've heard right, or heard anything. 3) When I try to act on those impressions, sometimes I forget, or I'm afraid to risk being wrong. 4) Sometimes "day after day, month after month, year after year" is exactly what I can't pull off.

Now what? To hone my skills of discernment, I also need time in the scriptures; talks with trustworthy friends; learning from mistakes; time to prioritize, plan, and evaluate; and lots and lots of practice. Some revelation comes only on a run, and often a run in the dark. Some revelation comes only when I'm still. Some revelation comes only when I've paid a price of personal sacrifice, hard work, deep healing, or giving up my usual haunts. Sometimes what I thought was revelation wasn't. Sometimes the stray thought I didn't think was revelation was. It can all feel a little overwhelming, especially when I see how much the world needs and how little I can do. *Now what?*

> *Do not be daunted*
> *by the enormity*
> *of the world's grief.*
> *Do justly, now.*
> *Love mercy, now.*
> *Walk humbly, now.*
> *You are not obligated*
> *to complete the work,*
> *but neither are you free*
> *to abandon it.*[8]

---

8. Rami Shapiro, *Wisdom of the Jewish Sages*, 41. Paraphrase of Rabbi Rami Shapiro's interpretive translation of Rabbi Tarfon's work on the Pirke Avot 2:15–16. The text is a commentary on Micah 6:8. https://www.chabad.org/library/article_cdo/aid/682513/jewish/English-Text.htm.

The privileges and responsibilities associated with the offices of the priesthood teach you and me how to let the Spirit empower us. Then they show us how to engage in God's work of empowering others.

Nourish body and soul. The office of deacon reminds us of our priesthood responsibility and privilege to nourish the world, distributing resources with equity and mercy. We need spiritual guidance to do so without becoming "daunted by the enormity of the world's grief" or simply justifying our excess. *Likewise*, the Holy Ghost can empower us more readily when we're not hungry and exhausted. Sure, fasting and prayer bring the Spirit close. Just skipping breakfast because we're not paying attention does not. Neither does watching *Law and Order* until 2:00 a.m., or calling it exercise to walk to the mailbox and back. Genuine nourishment to body and soul helps us be more in tune with the Spirit.

Build community. Teachers (rabbis) in ancient times used scriptural scholarship to help their communities live the law and get along. Today, women and men as teachers and Zion-builders can empower others as we ask inspired questions, facilitate learning from both mistakes and successes, and make it safe to be honest and open. *Likewise*, we connect with the Spirit more readily when our human connections are strong. The Spirit is alienated when we are alienated from others. It returns when we sincerely apologize, change, and forgive. We get more personal revelation when we're trying to help, serve, and empower others than when asking God to fix our problems.[9]

Rewrite the story. Priests must perform ordinances accurately so people can reliably imagine and seek God's promises. Temple ordinances we officiate in as women and men help others and us weave deliverance, redemption, and holiness into our stories of

---

9. A beautiful reminder from Joseph Grenny, personal correspondence.

sorrow, sin, and loss. *Likewise*, the sacrament and temple ordinances can help us picture the promises we've been given. They remind us to stop ruminating on the past and focus instead on how we've grown, not just how we've failed. They help us re-center on spiritual realities, experience beauty and rest, identify problems we need to address, recommit to values we want to live, and invite God close.

Ask eagerly. Elders are commissioned to confirm the Church with the Holy Ghost in all they do. Spiritually experienced women and men can participate in this work as we pray for, bless, and heal others in the Church, the family, and the world through the gifts of the Holy Ghost. *Likewise*, we grow in spiritual power when we show up each day to eagerly ask God how to be in His service, instead of asking sheepishly (if at all), "Is there anything you really need from me today? Because if you do, I'll certainly try to do it. No? Great, thank you, bye. Amen." We can afford to trust God enough to enthusiastically desire His will, praying with paper and pen in hand to capture and act on His promptings. When we consecrate our lives to His work each day, He consecrates His vast resources to help us each day. There will be enough and to spare.

Step up. High priests are charged with governing wards, stakes, missions, and temples. Women share in these important leadership duties, including in presidencies and in councils. When we prepare spiritually, we can step up with both confidence and compassion to positive organizational influence and power. We can raise concerns, offer suggestions, build on others' ideas, volunteer to help, represent the powerless, and invite the quiet to speak. *Likewise*, we grow in spiritual power as we first develop compassion for ourselves. The Holy Ghost can help give voice to the wounded and weary within us. He can quiet shame and blame and empower the wisest, most spiritually mature part of us to step up with confidence to the leadership of our souls. He can then help us be calm, curious, compassionate, and creative with others.

Empower others. Patriarchs and sealers help others identify their personal mission, create eternal relationships, and raise the next generation. Women and men participate in these roles as we develop the spiritual gift of prophecy, point out others' strengths and virtues, create and maintain loving families, and support the next generation of children, youth, converts, new missionaries, new move-ins, or new anything else. *Likewise*, we grow in spiritual power as we do the hard work of figuring out what we want most and what the Lord wants most for us and our personal mission. The Spirit will attend when we step into the adult role of helping empower the next generation by asking more than telling, listening more than talking, and watching more than showing.

Try again. Apostles and Seventies model the spiritual task of enduring to the end, never laying down their spiritual commissions but remaining fully engaged in God's work for the rest of their lives. To strengthen them in this weighty task, the Lord sends angels to bear them up and is personally in their midst. *Likewise*, we can join their commission as a lifelong disciple and witness of the Savior, and we can expect their rewards as a recipient of the ministering of angels and as a joint-heir with Christ of all that His Father has and is. Making our calling and election sure is less about never making another mistake and more about writing His love in our hearts and trying again when we fall. We can remember that things worth doing are worth doing badly, rather than not doing them at all, while we learn to do them better. When we take smart risks, practice the hard parts, and learn from mistakes, our confidence can wax strong in the presence of the Lord—not just because we feel the confidence to stand in His presence but because we gain full confidence that His presence, seen or unseen, felt or unfelt, is always with us (see D&C 121:45).

HEIRS OF THE POWER OF GOD

An heir is someone with rights to the wealth or position of another upon that person's death, or, by a definition I like even better, someone who inherits and continues the legacy of a predecessor. Under the second definition, heirs don't just get wealth or position to do with as they please. To continue a legacy, the heir must have acquired the skills, values, character, and goals of the "testator," the person who sets the terms of the will and leaves the legacy.

Our Father wants to bequeath upon us His most valuable assets—wisdom, virtue, character, and power. Like a testator who leaves a will, He sets the terms for inheriting. That determination is not based on just who He loves, for He loves us all. It must also be based on who is trustworthy with His all-encompassing power—who has the values, character, wisdom, and skill to use the inheritance for the ultimate good of all.

Some people think it is blasphemous to assume that we can become like God. Members of the restored Church of Christ might call it blasphemous to assume God either could not or would not pass all that He has and is on to His children. His power and goodness are so vast that He can raise us up, even from our weak and infantile state, to stand at His side, do what He does, love as He loves, even become as He is. God is not defined only by what He *possesses* that no one else has, but what He *bequeaths* to all who will qualify to receive it. God is not just unfathomably more than we are; He knows how to make *us* unfathomably more than we are. He is fully engaged in the holy work of raising the next generation, passing on a legacy of virtue, wisdom, and the power to generate spiritual life in others. This is the legacy we have the responsibility and the unimaginable privilege of preserving and passing on to those we love.

From Elder Bruce R. McConkie: "What, then, is the doctrine of the priesthood? And how shall we live as the servants of the Lord?

"This doctrine is that God our Father is a glorified, a perfected, and an exalted being who has all might, all power, and all dominion, who knows all things and is infinite in all his attributes, and who lives in the family unit. . . .

"It is that he has given us an endowment of heavenly power here on earth. . . . that we can enter an order of the priesthood named the new and everlasting covenant of marriage (see D&C 131:2), named also the patriarchal order, because of which order we can create for ourselves eternal family units of our own, patterned after the family of God our Heavenly Father.

"It is that we have power, by faith, to govern and control all things, both temporal and spiritual; to work miracles and perfect lives; to stand in the presence of God and be like him because we have gained his faith, his perfections, and his power, or in other words the fulness of his priesthood. . . .

"This is the power we can gain through faith and righteousness. . . .

"Truly there is power in the priesthood—a power which we seek to acquire to use, a power which we devoutly pray may rest upon us and upon our posterity forever."[10]

Elder McConkie goes on to quote the words of God to Isaiah, who writes: "As for me, this is my covenant with them, saith the Lord; My spirit that is upon thee, and my words which I have put in thy mouth, shall not depart out of thy mouth, nor out of the mouth of thy seed, nor out of the mouth of thy seed's seed, saith the Lord, from henceforth and for ever" (Isaiah 59:21).

Christ is the only legitimate heir to all the Father has, the only one whose perfect life meets all the terms of the Testator and qualifies Him to inherit all the Father has. That power would be unsafe in the hands of anyone without an unwavering commitment to

---

10. Bruce R. McConkie, "The Doctrine of the Priesthood," *Ensign*, May 1982.

the legacy of the Testator. Christ holds that inheritance in trust for each of us. If we are born again, adopted into His family, and willing to ceaselessly repent and grow until His laws are written on our hearts (see Hebrews 8:10), His Atonement can qualify us to inherit with Him. He becomes the mediator or the executor of the will, so that we "which are called might [also] receive the promise of eternal inheritance" (Hebrews 9:15).

Women do not need a separate female savior or exemplar of holiness. Christ possesses in full all the traits and spiritual skills of the perfect man and the perfect woman. Eventually Christ will not just bequeath to us all that our Father has, but all that our Mother has. Women and men may arrive at "the measure of the stature of the fulness of Christ" (Ephesians 4:13) from somewhat different paths, but these differences in experience and perspective can enrich and bless the whole as we eventually become both fully ourselves and fully at one in Christ.

Jesus Christ did not hold priesthood in ways recognized by the Sanhedrin, the center of priesthood power in His day. Women and men who seek priesthood power through His name today may or may not be recognized as having power or position in the world, or sometimes even at church. But with His authority and His Spirit, we can gain power to act in His name for the salvation of the human family. We can associate with angels. We can enter God's presence. When we do, we will walk into halls of power that exceed any earthly sovereignty—places accessible only through the gate of heaven.

Elder Jeffrey R. Holland shares his apostolic witness: "I testify of him, the Redeemer of the world and Master of us all. He is the Only Begotten Son of the living God, who has exalted that son's name over every other, and has given him principality, power, might, and dominion at his right hand in the heavenly place. We esteem this Messiah to be holy, harmless, undefiled—the bearer of unchangeable priesthood (see Heb. 7:24, 26). He is the anchor to our souls and our high priest of promise. He is our God of good things to come."[11]

Elder Neil L. Andersen states, "We are sons and daughters of heavenly parents who love us and who have sent us on a course to become more like them."[12] I look forward to the day when the priesthood power of those daughters can be envisioned with clarity along with that of those sons. Perhaps that day will fully arrive only when the veil is fully rent and the face of our Heavenly Mother as well as our Heavenly Father is fully revealed. But as women and men more clearly understand our life-giving responsibilities, authority, power, and privileges, perhaps we are a step closer to the fulfillment of Nephi's prophecy about us all: "And it came to pass that I, Nephi, beheld the power of the Lamb of God, that it descended upon the saints of the church of the Lamb, and upon the covenant people of the Lord, who were scattered upon all the face of the earth; and they were armed with righteousness and with the power of God in great glory" (1 Nephi 14:14).

Unlike power in the world that is amassed and held, power in the priesthood exists to be disseminated. God's power is a tree that bears fruit, and the fruit always bears seeds, and the seeds always have the potential to sprout. Women and men are each entitled to inherit God's priesthood power. Women and men are each integral and indispensable to the fulfillment and continuance of this legacy.

---

11. Jeffrey R. Holland, "Miracles of the Restoration," *Ensign,* May 1994.
12. Neil L. Andersen, "Looking Back and Looking Forward," *New Era,* August 2008.

INDEX

Aaronic Priesthood: power and authority of, 21; ordination of young men to, 52–53, 76; and family history work, 98; and ministering of angels, 103–7. *See also* Deacon(s); Priests; Teachers

Adam, 41, 51, 55, 58–59, 162–63n19

Adoption, 165

Adversity: community building through, 84–85; growth through, 112–13, 183–84

Andersen, Neil L., 194

Angels, ministering of, 103–7, 190

Animal symbols, 36–37

Anxiety, tolerating, 146–47

Apostasy, 45–46

Apostles, 169, 171–72, 190–91

Atonement: childbirth and understanding, 33–34; spiritual rebirth through, 157–59; blessings of, 175–77

Baker, Jenny Oaks, 58

Ballard, Melvin J., 138–39

Ballard, M. Russell: on availability of priesthood, 6; on blessings of keeping covenants, 12; on priesthood keys, 22; on women and priesthood authority, 25, 108; on blessings of priesthood, 27–28; on endowment, 91–92; on procreative and priesthood power, 160

Baptism: compared to mortal birth, 32–34; and fulfillment of Mosaic law, 91

Bednar, David A., 98

Benson, Ezra Taft, 40–42

Birth and childbirth: baptism compared to, 32–34; prayer and companionship during,

124–25; and sealing power, 162–66. *See also* Midwives; Spiritual rebirth

Bishops, 131–32

Blessings, for children, 116–17

"Born in the covenant," 163–66

Breast cancer, healing of woman with, 120

Brewerton, Ted E., 181–82

Burton, Linda K., 8–9, 26, 184–85

Burton, Theodore M., 163–64

Calling and election made sure, 190

Character, growing in, 16–19

Childbirth. *See* Birth and childbirth

Children: creating community for, 87; blessing, 116–17; parents' revelations concerning, 152–54; and raising next generation, 156–62, 190, 191–92; as heirs to priesthood power, 163–64; adopted, 165

Cholera, at Zion's Camp, 118–19

Clark, J. Reuben, 153, 159–60, 162–63n19

Clothing, 35

Community building: through food, 64–66; as responsibility of teachers, 70–71, 75–76, 188; in primitive church, 72–75; and false teachers, 77–78; through adversity, 84–85; love in, 85–87; examples of, 86–88

Confidence: of men versus women, 142–43; learning, 144–48

Confirmation: of new members, 110–11; of church, 111–13

Constraints, 183–84

Cook, Quentin L., 125–26

Councils, 135–36; skills to participate effectively in, 136–38; confidence in value of diversity in, 138–40; confidence in our contributions to, 140–47; confidence in Lord's willingness to inspire, 147–48

"Covenant, born in," 163–66

Covenant promises, 184–85

Covenant relationships, 44–46

Covenants: keeping, 9, 12; earnest on, 177–82

Criticism, 145–46

Cure, versus healing, 122, 123n15

Deacon(s): duties of, 50, 188; history of, 51–55; Jesus Christ as, 56–59; learn to see with new eyes, 60–61

Diakonos, 50

Discipleship, blessings of, 175–77

Diversity, confidence in value of, in councils, 138–40

Divorce, 102–3

Dweck, Carol, 146

Ears to hear, eyes to see and, 60–64

INDEX

Elders, 109, 110–23, 189
Elephant ride, 179–80
Empowerment, 66–69, 190
Endowment, 29–30, 35, 91–92
Enduring to the end, 190
Eternal family, authority and power to organize and administer, 162–66
Eve, 36, 41, 55, 58–59, 162–63n19
Experience, gaining spiritual power through, 112–13
Eyes to see and ears to hear, 60–64
Eyring, Henry B.: on keeping covenants, 9n8; on spirit world, 44; on limitations and humility, 49; on speaking and acting in God's name, 108; on parents and revelation, 152

Failure, fear of, 145–46
Faith: in just God, 5; building, 19; to be healed, 179; to heal, 179; to command natural world, 179–80; gift of exceedingly great, 181–82
False teachers, 77–78
Family: authority and power to organize and administer eternal, 162–66; authority presiding in, 167
Family history work, 97–103, 168. *See also* Angels, ministering of
Fear, 167–68

Fellowshipping, 86–87, 112–13
Food, serving, 49–51; women's role in, 54–55; godly role of, 55–56; and Jesus Christ as deacon, 56–59; and gratitude, 59–60; need for eyes to see and ears to hear in, 60–64; and relationship building, 64–66; divine commission concerning, 66–69
Foster children, 156

Gender roles: seeming unfairness concerning, 4–6; and priesthood power, offices, and authority, 21–25; and confidence in councils, 140–43
Genealogy, 97–103, 168
God: as fair and just, 4–5; becoming like, 7–8, 26–28, 44, 191–92; role of, in bringing priesthood power into our lives, 16; inheriting power of, 43–44, 191–94; feeds humankind, 55–56; love of, 85–86; speaking and acting in name of, 108; faith in willingness of, to inspire councils, 147–48; as example of parenthood, 160–61
Godly power, pattern for conveying, 67–68
Grant, Heber J., 62n7
Gratitude, 59–60
Groupthink, 139–40

INDEX

Hartley, William G., 62n7, 76n6
Hawn's Mill Massacre, 179
Healey, Martha, 180
Healing: blessings of, 117–23; methods for, 123–25; learning art of, 125–27; and gift of faith to be healed, 179; and gift of faith to heal, 179
Heart surgeries, 17–18
High priests, 130, 131–32, 189–90. *See also* Leadership and government
Hinckley, Gordon B., 112
Holiness: growing in, 16–19; Jesus Christ as example of, 193–94
Holland, Jeffrey R., 105–6, 193–94
Holy Ghost: role of, in bringing priesthood power into our lives, 15; and priesthood power, 25–26; speaking by power of, 106; confirmation of newly baptized with, 110–11; confirming church with, 111–13, 189; ordination of others according to gifts of, 113; leading meetings by, 113–15; intercession of, in prayer, 120–21; as God's "earnest money" on promises of eternity, 177–82; privilege of daily manifestations from, 185; and connection with others, 188; nourishment and being in tune with, 188; confidence to lead through, 189–90. *See also* Spiritual power
Holy Temple Visitors' Center, 93
Humility, 49, 110

Influence, 6–7
Inheritance, 43–44
Injustice, 4–6
Intimacy, 84–85
Israel, 160–61, 169–71

Jerusalem, nourishment of Saints in, 49–50
Jesus Christ: role of, in bringing priesthood power into our lives, 15; learning about, through symbols, 30–39; understands our pain, 37–39; order of, 39–43; becoming joint heirs alongside, 43–44, 191–94; power of, 43–44; priesthood held by, 52; and preparation, blessing, and distribution of food, 54; as deacon, 56–59; and miracle of loaves and fishes, 57–58, 60; serves disciples, 67; as teacher, 73–74, 81, 83–84; visit of, to Americas, 74, 83–84, 121; love of, 85–86; as great high priest, 90–91; healing methods of, 123–24; and healing of woman with issue of blood, 125–26; as example of parenthood, 160–62; Apostles and Seventies as witnesses of, 169–72; taking upon name of,

INDEX

173–74; women as witnesses of, 174–75; and blessings of discipleship, 175–77; fulness of joy of, 176; commanding through name of, 180; waxing strong in presence of, 190–91. *See also* Atonement

Joy, fulness of Christ's, 176

Justice, 4–6

Keltner, Dacher, 133–34

Kimball, Camilla Eyring, 117–18n11

Kimball, Edward, 117–18n11

Kimball, Spencer W., 117–18n11

Kindness, 72

Kirtland Temple, dedicatory prayer for, 112

Knowledge, gift of, 178–79

Law of Moses, 51–52, 54, 90, 91

Leadership and government, 129–32; paradox of power in, 132–35; and effective use of councils, 135–48; confidence in, through Holy Ghost, 189–90

Lewis, C. S., 31

Limitations, 49

Loaves and fishes, miracle of, 57–58, 60

Love: manifesting, 10n10; and community building, 85–87

Lung cancer, prayers for woman with, 121–22

Martinez, Hugo, 177–78

Mary, 152–53

McConkie, Bruce R., 192

McCune, Elizabeth, 180–81

Meetings. *See* Councils

Meetings, leading, by Holy Ghost, 113–15

Melchizedek, 40

Melchizedek Priesthood, 20–21, 39–41, 52, 109–10. *See also* Apostles; Elders; High priests; Patriarchs; Sealers; Seventies

Midwives, 35, 178–79

Ministering of angels, 103–7, 190

Miracles, gift of, 177–78

Missionary work, 115–16, 181

Moroni, 44–45, 147

Mortality, 16–17, 154–57

Moses, 169–71

Natural world, gift of faith to command, 179–80

Nauvoo Relief Society, 78–79

Nelson, Russell M.: on living beneath privileges, 11; as example of growing in spiritual power, 17–18; on women using priesthood authority, 108; on need for women of power, 127–28; on serving with Lord's authority and power, 132–33; on apostles, 172; on receiving revelation, 186

New members, empowering, 110–11

INDEX

Next generation, raising, 156–62, 190, 191–92
Nourishing others. *See* Food, serving

Oaks, Dallin H.: on priesthood, 20; on priesthood keys, 22; on priesthood authority of women, 24; on becoming like heavenly parents, 44; on women's performance of priesthood ordinances, 94–95; on authority of women missionaries, 115; on women's role in priesthood, 159–60; on authority presiding in family, 167; on taking upon name of Jesus Christ, 173–74
Oath and covenant of the priesthood, 26–27, 43–46
Okazaki, Chieko, 37–39
Options, limited, 183–84
Ordaining others, as duty of elders, 113
Order of the Son of God, 39–43
Ordinances: and spiritual progression, 27, 30; of confirmation of new members, 110–11; blessings of, 188–89. *See also* Temple ordinances
Oscarson, Bonnie L., 184

Packer, Boyd K.: on living beneath privileges, 11; on priesthood authority and power, 23; on sealing power, 150; on family history work, 168; on duties of Seventy and Twelve, 171n1
Pain, Jesus Christ's understanding of, 37–39
Parenthood, 156, 159–60
Past, accepting, 158
Patriarchal blessings, 151–52, 153–54
Patriarchal order, 150–51
Patriarchs, 149–51; duties of, 150, 190; and gifts of revelation, vision, and prophecy, 151–54; women as, 154–55; as fathers, 166–67
Patton, George S., 103
Perfectionism, 146
Perry, Virginia, 86–87
Pilcomayo River flood, 181–82
Pinegar, Ed J., 19
Planning, gaining confidence through, 144–45
Power: in world versus priesthood, 6–8; paradox of, 132–35. *See also* Priesthood power
Prayers, for sick, 117–23, 124
Preaching, gift of, 180–81
Premortal world, 154–56, 162n19
Pride, 110
Priesthood: women's ordination to, 4–6; power in world versus, 6–8; oath and covenant of, 26–27, 43–46; empowerment through, 66–69; roles associated with, 95–96; doctrine and power of, 192

INDEX

Priesthood authority: versus priesthood power, 8–9; conferral of, 9, 20–25; defined, 9; women's use of, 108–9; of women missionaries, 115; to create eternal families, 162–66

Priesthood blessings, for children, 116–17

Priesthood keys, conferral of priesthood authority through, 20–25

Priesthood offices, 21–22, 50, 74. *See also* Apostles; Bishops; Deacon(s); Elders; High priests; Patriarchs; Priests; Sealers; Seventies; Teachers (priesthood office)

Priesthood power: versus priesthood authority, 8–9; defined, 9; use of, 9–10; living up to privileges of, 10–13; development of, 14; operation of, 14–15; individual roles in, 15–16; and growing in character and holiness, 16–19; through spiritual tutoring, 25–26; blessings of, 26–28; learning through temple ordinances and growing in, 30–39; skills and attributes of, 59–69; principles and blessings of, associated with Melchizedek Priesthood, 109–10

Priesthood titles, 50

Priests, 89–90; duties of, 90, 188–89; history of, 90–92; in ancient temple, 93; and endowment with priestly identity, 93–94; and sacrament prayer, 96–97; and family history work, 97–103; and ministering of angels, 107

Primary child, solution for wandering, 129–31

Primary teachers, and successful missionary work, 115–16

Procreation, 159–60

Prophecy, 151–54, 177–78

Rabbis, 73

Rebirth, spiritual, 157–59, 161

Relationship building, through food, 64–66. *See also* Community building

Relief Society, 78–79, 103–4

Renlund, Dale G., 136–38, 177–78

Renlund, Ruth Lybbert, 136–38

Repentance, 16

Resilience, 145–46

Revelation, 151–55, 174, 186–87

Righteousness, importance of, in living up to privileges, 42–43

Russell, Bill, 146–47

Sacrament: author imitates, as child, 3–4, 13; symbolism of, 34–35; passing, 53–54, 60–61, 62n7; and eyes to see and ears to hear, 60–61; women's involvement in, 61–62; and fulfillment of Mosaic law, 91; participation in blessing,

96–97; and taking upon name of Jesus Christ, 173–74
Sacrifice(s): in building faith and spiritual power, 19; in childbirth, 33–34; animal, 36–37; made by men, 37; in parenthood, 161. *See also* Atonement
Scott, Richard G., 79–80, 110, 112–13
Sealers, 150–51, 190
Sealing, of author's grandparents, 99–101
Sealing power, 150, 162–66
Self-confidence: of men versus women, 142–43; learning, 144–48
September 11, 2001 terrorist attacks, 101
Service, need for eyes to see and ears to hear in, 60–64. *See also* Food, serving
Setting apart, 113
Seventies, 169–71, 190–91
Sick, praying for, 117–23. *See also* Healing
Sister missionaries, 65, 115, 181
Skarda, Carrie, 75
Smith, Alma, 179
Smith, Amanda, 179
Smith, Emma, 77, 113, 124
Smith, Hyrum, 118–19, 149–50
Smith, Joseph: on faith and justice, 5; on manifesting love, 10n10; on living beneath privileges, 11–12; on organization of human family, 46, 164; and vision of human family, 46, 164; on ordinances, 89; on kingdom of priests, 95; on ministering of angels, 103–4; and healing of sick, 118–19; heals Emma, 124; on revelation, 174
Smith, Joseph F., 20, 104–5, 117n11, 155–56
Smith, Joseph Fielding, 28, 94–95, 179
Smith, Julina L., 179
Smith, Lucy Mack, 72, 119
Snow, Eliza R., 180
Snow, Lorenzo, 185
Spiritual gifts, 125, 177–82
Spiritual power: gaining, 19, 112–13, 189, 190; and priesthood authority, 23–24; ordinances and growth in, 27, 30; humility and, 110. *See also* Holy Ghost
Spiritual progression, 7–8, 26–28
Spiritual rebirth, 157–59, 161
Strangers, love for, 85–87
Students, as teachers, 78–81
Symbols, 30–39

"Tabernacle of the congregation," 169–70
Talmage, James E., 150–51
Teachers: false, 77–78; students as, 78–81; powerful and empowering, 81–84
Teachers (priesthood office): duties of, 70–72, 188; in

primitive church, 72–75; role of, 75–77
Teaching: in primitive church, 72–75; importance of, in Church, 76–77
Teaching moments, 80–81
Teamwork, 135–48
Temple ordinances: and growing in spiritual power, 29–30; learning through, 30–39; women authorized to perform, 39–43, 91–92, 94–97; and blessings of oath and covenant of the priesthood, 43–46; performed by priests, 90; misunderstanding of, 91; and family history work, 97–103, 168; and ministering of angels, 107
Temple sacrifices, 91
Testosterone, 143
Tongue of angels, 106
Tongues, gift of speaking in and interpretation of, 180
Touch, importance of, 116
Tragedy, 85
Trials. *See* Adversity

Uchtdorf, Dieter F., 11
Unanimity, in councils, 141–42

Vision: of human family, 46, 164; developing gift of, 151–55

Water, turned to wine, 57n6
Weakness, 16–19, 25–26, 49
Well-being, knowledge of family history's impact on, 101–3
Whitney, Elizabeth Ann, 79
Widows, 49–50, 63
Widtsoe, John A., 30, 151–52
Wine, water turned to, 57n6
Woman with issue of blood, healing of, 125–26, 179
World, power in priesthood versus, 6–8
World War I, 103
Wright, Alicyn, 145
Wyoming elementary school siege, 104

Young, Brigham, 10–11, 46, 164
Young, Zina, 180
Young men, as priesthood holders, 52–53, 76. *See also* Aaronic Priesthood
Young women, bake bread for sacrament, 61–62

Zion's Camp, 118–19